MODERN IND...
Vegetarian C...

MODERN INDIAN
Vegetarian Cuisine

CHEF ANUJ SOOD

First published in India in 2023 by:
Chef Anuj Sood

Copyright © 2023 Chef Anuj Sood

Publishing facilitation: AuthorsUpFront

All rights reserved. No part of this publication may be reproduced, stored in a retrieval system, or transmitted, in any form or by any means, without the prior written permission of the AUTHOR, or as expressly permitted by law, or under terms agreed with the appropriate reprographic rights organisations. Enquiries concerning reproduction outside the scope of the above should be sent to the AUTHOR.

CONTENTS

Foreword vii
Testimonials viii
Introduction xii
Achievements and Laurels xvi
Traditional Kitchen Equipment xviii
Aesthetics of Plating xxi
Back to Basics xxiii
Basic Indian Curry Pastes xxv
Marinades xxvii
Gravies and Sauces xxxi
Spices and Herbs xxxviii
Pickles xlii

Starters 01
Salads 21
Soups 41
Main Course 55
Breads 105
Desserts 115

Measurement Table 128
Glossary 133
Acknowledgement 139
My Journey in Arabic Cuisine 140

FOREWORD

The ancient sacred literature of the *Vedas* enshrines a holistic and poetic cosmic vision. They represent the oldest, the most carefully nurtured, the most elaborately systematised and the most lovingly preserved oral tradition in the annals of the world. Unique in their perspective of time and space, their evocative poetry is, 'a joyous and spontaneous affirmation of life and nature'.

The *Vedic* seers regarded the Earth as a 'sacred space' for the consecrated endeavours and aspirations of humankind and for the practice of restraint and responsibility. This affirmative view of the inviolable sacred space in human consciousness is integral to the *Vedas* and the *Upanishads*.

Vegetarianism is a celebration of life and on all festive occasions Chefs outdo each other with a sense of positive competitiveness to create marvels of vegetarian cuisine.

Anuj, in my opinion, is one of most talented Chefs of his generation, a jewel amongst his peers. Meticulous, efficient, clean, hygienic, creative and his plates are a poetry or a song of taste and wonder.

His belief –
Earth is my mother, I am her son.
It represents for the world a Renaissance of the Third Plate.
What is good for the Earth is good for Humanity (Chefs and Guests).

My very best wishes for his success and his marvellous book debut!

Diwan Gautam Anand
Founding Trustee Cuisine India Foundation

TESTIMONIALS

What a great book, "Modern Indian Vegetarian Cuisine" designed for people who appreciate quality dishes that are easy to make, with a variety of flavours and tastes depending on which recipe you choose. Or if you care about what goes into your meals.

My association with Chef Anuj is since 2004, when he joined as Sous Chef at ITC Sheraton, New Delhi. I remember, when I was evaluating his skills, his dish was well balanced in all aspects, spices and taste. Seeing his confidence, I told him 'sky is the limit'.

Anuj takes charge! I was given the responsibility for the event, "India @60" in New York, USA. He assisted me as he accompanied me to New York to serve cocktails bites and dinner for 2,000 guests. The whole team enjoyed working under his charge. Anuj was always ready to accept challenges while working on new concepts such as Dehlvi—food from Delhi, Royal Vega—honestly vegetarian food on the guidelines of Ayurveda.

Anuj is a good professional and an eternal student. Our association working together for six years is the most memorable time of a mentor and a mentee.

Anuj is humble, has quite a positive attitude but takes very seriously on critical feedback and improves them with his team. Laid down standards and recipes are Bible for his executions.

The unique features of this book, besides dealing with spices, other ingredients and cooking methods of various delectable recipes in an easy yet simple ways are its attractive photographic presentation and that it is a vegetarian's delight. Anuj has demonstrated an in-depth knowledge about the art of cooking, while catering to foodies who look for plant-based recipes. I must add that his dishes and style of cooking takes the stress out of cooking.

I wish you all the best with your book and future endeavours!

Chef Manjit Singh Gill
President of the Indian Federation of Culinary Associations

TESTIMONIALS

My connection to Chef Anuj, began in 2010 in Dubai when I was looking for new talent as Chef de Cuisine for our Award-winning Indian restaurant, Ashiana in Dubai.

Within a short time of only two days, he cooked up a storm of delicious traditional and contemporary influenced food varieties inspired from the Indian subcontinent. We witnessed a great variety of vegetarian and non-vegetarian menu options with a large-scale portfolio of different spice levels, always flavourful and with the right consistency, simply spot on.

This was the beginning of a two-year journey, where Chef Anuj and myself worked together on different projects besides Ashiana, where he picked up the offered role. He managed to lead his team to great success, due to his cooking skills and humble, friendly personality.

For this book I really like the scenario of the contemporary plating and the freshness of the products just prepared or cooked as needed to the point. This with special regards to healthy requirements of vegetarian Indian food.

Chef Anuj, I wish you all the best with your new book and hopefully, our paths will cross again in the future.

Chef Martin Braecker

TESTIMONIALS

I first met Chef Anuj when he came for an interview to be a member of my "Culinary Development" team for Qatar Airways in 2011. It was a challenging, high-profile job, but I was confident that Anuj would adapt from his hotel background and work well with other in-flight Chefs.

I quickly identified the passion Chef Anuj had and employed him without hesitation. I was not disappointed as he was completely professional, dedicated and talented when it came to cooking and creating new, innovative regional menus.

As you will see from the dishes Chef Anuj has created for this book, they are exciting, appealing and look very appetising. The book is well laid out, colourful and easy to follow. I am very proud to know and have worked with Chef Anuj and am very happy to see him grow and expand his culinary knowledge and share it with you through this excellent book.

Culinary Regards,
Colin Binmore (retired); 45 years a Chef

TESTIMONIALS

Anuj Sood has been a go getter from the time he joined my FnB team in ITC hotels. From his college days he was a bright and upcoming chef. He has a flair for cooking, trying out interesting presentations and was always in a perfectionist mode to deliver the best. His passion for Indian cuisine is ceremonial.

He has worked on various cuisines and themed menus for large and important caterings. His cooking techniques too bring out the best flavours since they are unique as he likes to get to the bottom of the dish, its origin and other nuances attached.

Even when I travelled to his native place in Shimla, he introduced me to the finest Himachali cuisine. I wish him all the success with his new passion of creating a culinary experience via his book.

Raj Kamal Chopra
Corporate Chef, Fortune Park Hotels Ltd, Gurgaon

INTRODUCTION

The culinary journey has been a dream. Sometimes, I pinch myself reminiscing how and when I started and where I am now. It wasn't necessarily a logical progression, but I have had a deep interest in food and now a career to thank for. I consider myself fortunate to have discovered cooking when and where I did, as I have been able to witness and be part of the evolution of Indian food into what it is today – world class, simple and always inspiring!

I belong to a vegetarian family. I remember my childhood days; food played a very important role in our upbringing as it brought all the family members together to sit and share a meal. The delicious dishes served were always relished by all and the appreciative comments would further boost my mother's morale to cook lovingly for her family. I personally believe a touch of love and joy always takes the dish to the next level.

My culinary career started in 2001, after I joined the Institute of Hotel Management (IHM) Bengaluru, India. The experience gained and the cooking techniques taught at college piqued my interest, which helped me to pursue a career in cooking and become a chef. Being among the Top 10 in the country, I was selected through campus interviews to join the ITC Welcomgroup Management Institute, one of the premier institutes of the country. Thereafter, I further honed my skills in International and Indian cooking and worked with various master chefs in Luxury Collection ITC Hotels across India.

My first assignment was in Sheraton Hotel, New Delhi, as Banquet Chef in 2006, where I was fortunate to work with mentors like Chef Manisha Bhasin, Rajkamal Chopra, Manjit Singh Gill, Gautam Anand among many others. I then represented ITC Welcomgroup at India@60 Event in September 2007, New York, where I was part of the team and gained experience of cooking for international events. I was even the Final Nominee as Young Chef of the Year 2009, an event conducted by a leading Indian daily, *Hindustan Times*.

Introduction

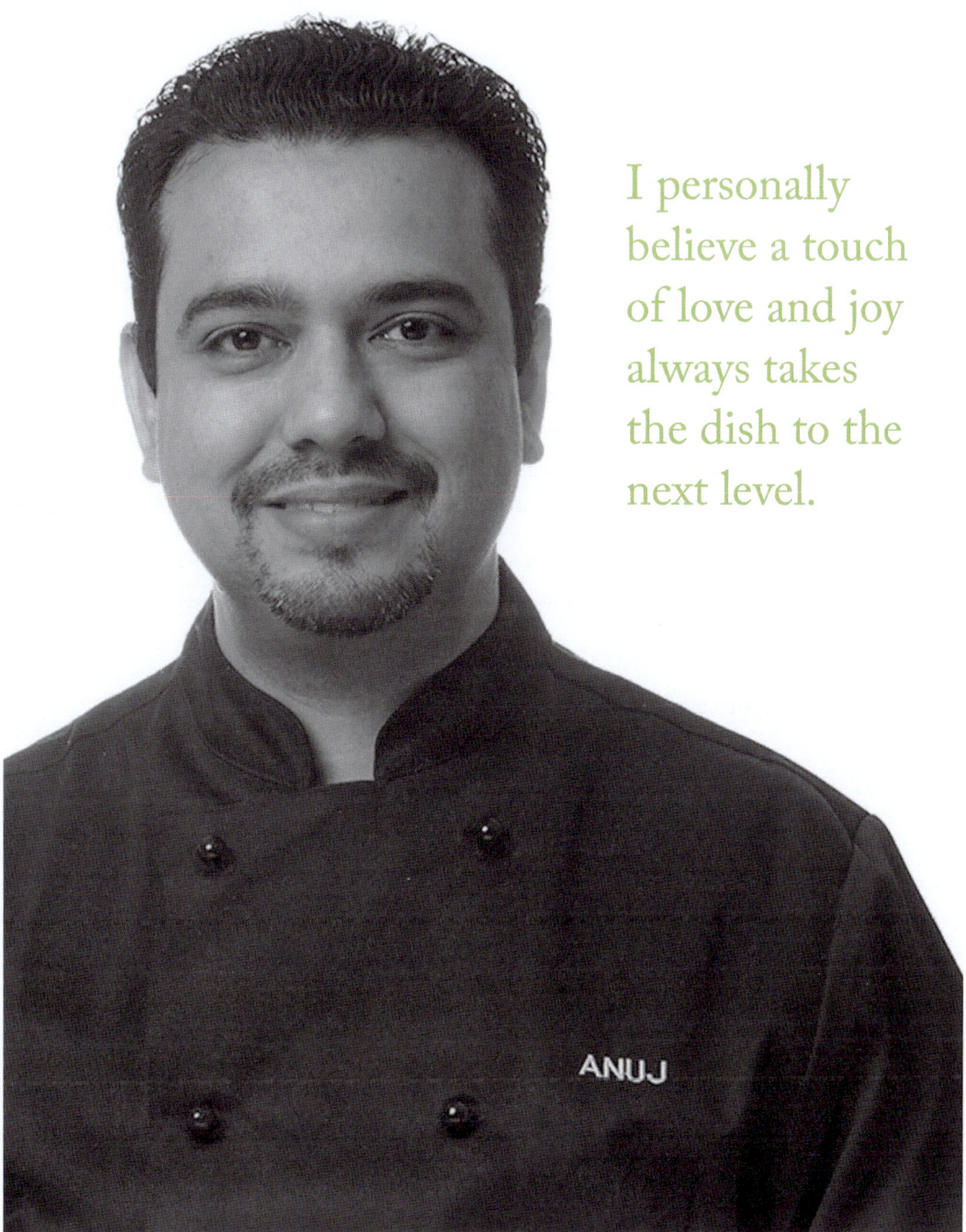

I personally believe a touch of love and joy always takes the dish to the next level.

I take immense pride in sharing with you all, what and where I am today. It is because of the efforts of all my mentors with whom I met at various phases of my life. Being an Indian and growing up with its rich cultural heritage and multicuisine degustation choices, I have been fortunate to work with Master Chefs like Imtiaz Quereshi and Mohammad Rais Qureshi to further enhance the repertoire of Indian food. With age and experience, I realised it was time to venture abroad and explore new culinary treasures.

My gastronomic international journey began in Dubai in March 2010. It was then that my outlook towards life and career completely changed as I realised that Indian cuisine has a lot of potential. Even though Indian dishes have a few complicated and very technical aspects, it needs to be refined while keeping the authenticity intact when serving to woo your customers.

I organised various food festivals during my period in Dubai, innovating the menu each time by including dishes from all over India which were highly appreciated by the guests. Executive Chef Martin Braecker helped me in plating the regional dishes in a contemporary way, which definitely changed my outlook.

In 2011, I joined the Qatar Airways as the Development Chef, which provided me with opportunities to further explore the world and travel across almost 40 countries to curate onboard recipes, while exploring regional cuisines from all over the world. It also gave me a chance to work alongside Michelin starred chefs like Nobu Matsuhisa, Tom Aitkens and Ramzi Choueiri. It was this kind of exposure that gave me innovative ideas to develop recipes for the Airlines with culinary legends. Adopting traditional ways, I even learnt Arabic style of cooking food while working in the Middle East. My sound foundation in understanding spices further helped me design Arabic recipes for the Airlines, and I conducted various workshops for chefs catering for these flights across the world.

My desire to explore the world continued as I joined Hyatt Regency Hotel in Sydney. I was responsible for handling the entire banquet spreads and I did some major events. Finally, I settled in Melbourne and joined the Qantas, catering meals for their flights and still continue to explore new recipes while working with a team of chefs from Rockpool.

Introduction

> The selection of recipes featured in this book are just a few amazing ones that I love to cook for my family. These are easily approachable and presentable, and you will find dishes that are perfect for special occasions and celebrations.

This book is to inspire young chefs to think of creative ways to use colourful ingredients and spices in different ways to present Indian food in an innovative, contemporary way. I have complied a host of classic and regional comfort dishes and ultimate family favourites, which of course has taken me eight years to publish and share it with the world. I guarantee that these vegetarian recipes will not only tickle your taste buds, but the meals are wholesome and totally balanced that will help you revive, enliven and energise. The selection of recipes featured in this book are just a few amazing ones that I love to cook for family. These are easily approachable and presentable, and you will find dishes that are perfect for special occasions and celebrations.

- https://www.facebook.com/soodgastronomy
- https://www.instagram.com/soodgastronomy/

Bon appetite!

ACHIEVEMENTS AND LAURELS

Designed and implemented food and beverage service concept (New Frontiers) for Qatar Airways Business and Economy Class.

Represented as Qatar Airways Culinary Ambassador for network wide flight routes for over 160 destinations.

Responsible for Modern International food design, workshops and menu planning for Qatar Airways.

Launch of Michelin Star Chef concept in Qatar Airways for its First and Business class cabins.

Worked with Michelin star chefs Nobu Matsuhisa, Tom Aikens and Ramzi. Implementation of Michelin star chef's dishes onboard.

Qualified Level 2 with Merit from WSET (Wine and Spirit Education Trust).

Team member of pre-opening team of Jumeirah Etihad Towers Abu Dhabi (flagship properties of Jumeirah group).

Conducted food festivals for various regional and international cuisines in Sheraton Dubai Creek and Towers.

Represented Sheraton Dubai Creek Hotel in Food and Beverage Academy held in November 2010.

Final Nominee as Young Chef of the Year by *Hindustan Times* in 2009.

Youngest chef to represent the country and ITC Ltd in "India@60" event held in September 2007, New York, USA.

Certified Six Sigma Green Belt.

Leader of area effectiveness team for Banquets in ITC Hotels.

Brand custodian of vegetarian food for ITC Hotels.

Achievements and Laurels

Won many medals in chef competitions held at Pragati Maidan, New Delhi, India.

Published articles on food in leading Indian, Australian and Dubai newspapers.

Have been invited for various television (TV) shows in leading Indian channels, Dubai Mega Mela, Qatar International Food Festival and Dubai channels.

Managed and participated in live cooking demonstrations at the Qatar Airways Cooking Theatre at QIFF: 2013, 2014 and 2015.

Cooking shows I have been featured in:
- Foodie; with Kunal Vijayker, January, 2010
- Dubai One, July, 2010
- Star News, April, 2009
- AajTak, October, 2009
- Zee News, September 2009
- NDTV, December, 2008

TRADITIONAL KITCHEN EQUIPMENT

Key characteristics:
- Huge and heavy;
- Copper or brass;
- Lined with tin to prevent any reaction with food;
- Narrow in the neck to trap heat and flavours/especially for *dum* (slow) cooking;
- Use firewood as one of the best heat sources;
- Charcoal is another great source of traditional fuel which gives great results.

Bhagona: Or the *patili* (pot) is made of brass with a lid. Used for *bhuna* or sauté or even for boiling and simmering.

Deg/Degchi: Pear-shaped pot with a lid made of either brass, copper or aluminium. The shape of this utensil is ideally suited for *dum* cooking; for example, pulao, biryani, etc.

Kadhai: A deep concave utensil made of brass and iron, used for deep or stir frying.

Lagan: It is a round and shallow copper utensil with a slightly concave bottom. It is very commonly used in high volume kitchens and Northern India.

Mahi Tawa: It is the Awadh version of the griddle-shaped like a big round, flat bottomed tray with raised edges used for cooking kebabs.

Seeni: It is a big *thali* (plate) used to cover lagan or mahi tawa when heat is applied from above by putting pieces of burning charcoal on the top.

Charoti/Baltoi: Heavy bottomed and narrow neck cooking pot primary used in banquet functions in Himachal and Andhra Pradesh. An empty Charoti weighs about 30-35 kgs. Food cooked in these Charoties is most delicious.

Urlai: Heavy bottom cooking pot with integrated handles, commonly used in southern India, the shape itself gives more surface area for food to breathe and develop its flavour.

Modern Indian Vegetarian Cuisine

AESTHETICS OF PLATING

Indian food traditionally is more about its taste as compared to the look of the dish or its plating. However, in this evolving industry one always enjoys and tastes food with all his senses. Plating is integral part of the food and completes the dish.

Indian cuisine is very colourful, ranging from its spices to starch to the vegetables that allows the culinary professionals to elevate the food. I always compare the plating of the food like a blank canvas and every time we plate, we create a beautiful edible picture.

It took me good seven to eight years of cooking experience in traditional food to change my mindset to adopt this art. While working with master chefs and in the ITC Hotels we always focused on the taste and the recipe, as we knew the dish would be served in a standard bowl or a chaffing dish for a buffet spread. I still remember when I was a Junior Sous Chef in the Indian banquet kitchen ITC Welcomhotel Saket, we were required to cook for a competition to display a cold-plated food and the best dish would be judged. After finishing a fourteen-hour long shift, I started with my dish for the competition. I had planned to make *Aam Ke Jamun* (gulab jamun shaped like a mango and stuffed with mangoes) and plate the dish. After practicing for nearly five hours, I prepared the final dish, it was almost 3:00 am in the night by the time I got to the plating of the dish. By then, I was totally exhausted and I was out of creative ideas on plating, so I decided to take a quick break to freshen up and start again at 4:00 am.

For plating, I took two pieces of the jamun. I cut the first piece into two. The second piece as a whole was put on the plate and garnished with mint leaves to show them as leaves of a mango. I did my best to make it as presentable as I could and then went to the lockers for a short break. It was almost 8.00 am by the time I finalised my dish. The Executive Chef who reviewed my dish, applauded my efforts, but my plate did not make it to the final list for the competition. I was quite disappointed, so I rushed to see my plate, and when I did, I saw that it had become mushy and soggy, and looked like a disaster. My idea had failed. My boss later called me in his office, she acknowledged my efforts and encouraged me to practice more. This motivated me to further hone my skills, as I continued to

Modern Indian Vegetarian Cuisine

learn and work with Martin Braecker, originally from Germany, who gave me a whole new outlook on plating techniques.

In time and armed with new knowledge and experiences, we changed the whole restaurant menu in Sheraton Hotel, Dubai. I developed my own little tips and tricks to understand the basics and started treating food presentation as an art. It took a lot of time, practice, equipment and expertise to understand and develop finesse for plating of food.

I have shared few basic plating concepts that may be practiced to hone your skills and can be easily adopted by amateur as well as home cooks.

BACK TO BASICS

Plates: Style, design and size of a plate are an essential aspect of plating, however it is a personal choice whether to follow any trend or an established brand or be creative by making your own signature style. The portion of food and its plating style should determine the right size of a plate; for example, a plate may be big, however half of it is used for pattern and rest half for plating a portion of the food. I personally avoid dishes with large bespoke patterns on the rim as then these patterns pull attention away from the food.

You need to be wise in your selections and consider factors such as ease of eating, durability, dishwasher safe, etc.

Grazing bowls, frying pans, copper pans, spoons, glasses are other alternatives that may be used for plating of food, it all depends on personal choices, however, again these should be practical and safe.

Tongs: Kitchen tongs are such a useful tool to have in the kitchen. If you don't have a pair, you should go out and even buy a few.

Moulds: A ring, square, diamond or any shape of a mould is especially handy when it comes to plating. It gives one an opportunity to present food in a circular style on the plate, which, when coupled with circular plates, adds to the symmetry of the dish.

Mesh sieve or fine strainer: A mesh or a strainer is an essential tool. It helps you to remove lumps from sauces and you can dust fine flavourful powdered spices on a plate.

Tweezer: This tool is easily available in food equipment stores as it is one of the best things to use by avoiding your fingers and use tweezers to finish the fine herb garnishes with precision. It works best when you have thick sausage fingers and it also helps to avoid any handprints on a plate.

I remember buying my first tweezer from a shaving shop in India for just Rs. 10 and I still have it. However, I would suggest that you should buy more professional ones.

Squeeze bottles: This is another item that I consider mandatory that a chef should always have. Keep a different a set of squeeze bottles, as these are good for holding purees, sauces, oils, etc., and will allow for those nice precision designs that you see.

Wet wipes/chux: When you are serving large number plates it is always advisable to have these handy to clean food smudges on bowls, plates or serving equipment.

Theory: Plating food is essentially an artistic exercise. But, if you are like me and you don't have an artistic bone in your body, then there are a few guidelines that can nudge you in the right direction.

Symmetry vs Asymmetry: Symmetry is when objects look the same even after you rotate them or see the reflection in a mirror, while asymmetry would be the opposite—if you rotate or reflect something and it doesn't look the same. This principle helps you to compose a plate by creating imaginary lines to then follow a pattern in a symmetrical manner that everyone likes. A neat plating is the first step for beginners, however asymmetrical plating are visible in Michelin star restaurants which requires practice and experience.

Negative Space and Portion Size: Portion size is very important, so stick to basics of portion sizes and similarly for platter portions. I am sure we don't want our food to go waste. Try and stick to odd numbers as much as possible as our brain likes 1, 3, 5, generally for some reasons. It is important to include negative space in your dish because it gives your eyes and brain a chance to process the plate of food in front of you.

When the food fills the plate from rim to rim, your brain has a hard time making out what is what and just sort of clumps it all together. Give your brain a break and help it understand what is happening by leaving some room.

Dish design: When designing a dish, always remember colour combinations, seasonality and availability as well as flavours as these should combine perfectly with each other as a whole. The dish blends beautifully with the use of colourful vegetables and sauce, which should be smooth and not too oily.

Garnish: A good garnish helps to complete the dish and adds a flare of freshness that appeals to the eye. Try and complement the dish with a choice of garnish that is edible and brings fineness to the dish.

- Fresh herbs
- Micro herbs
- Ginger juliennes
- Bell pepper curls
- Edible flowers
- Crisps of vegetables (okra, carrots, potato)
- Tomato juliennes and cherry tomatoes

This is just a basic guide for beginners. There are no boundaries to what can be done therefore be open to new ideas and practice to build your own unique style. When preparing dishes for the restaurant or for special occasions, always review the number guests, staffing and labour cost as these should all be factored in during plating. It is good to cross boundaries but with the budget and costing in mind.

BASIC INDIAN CURRY PASTES

You may find innumerable recipes in different books, but here is my own version with a twist to make perfect curry pastes.

Ginger Garlic Paste: This is the most commonly used paste in Indian cooking, the ratio and grinding are quite important. The ratio should be 1:4, one part ginger and four parts garlic. Grinding it in a mixer helps in making a smooth paste, which is equally good, however it comes out best if done in a traditional stone grinder. When you feel the paste between your fingers, it should feel slimy.

Ginger: 1 part
Garlic: 4 parts

Add enough water to make a smooth paste.

Boiled Onion Paste: Peel the onions and boil with whole spices – cardamom and cinnamon. Before you grind the mix, remove the spices to avoid dark colour. This paste is best for light thin curries/sauces/gravies.

Brown Onion Paste: Browning of onions is again an art, though readymade products available in the market has made our job much simpler. This paste can be used in thickening of curries/sauces/gravies.

Cashew Nut Paste: This is a very basic paste used in every Indian kitchen. Use broken pieces of cashew nut as it is always cost effective. Ensure that the cashew nuts are pre-soaked or these can be boiled before grinding into a paste. Depending on the usage, it works as a thickening agent in most Indian curries or in kebabs for marination.

Almond Paste: It is very similar to a cashew nut paste, it is used as a thickening agent for curries and often added in kebabs for marination.

Raw Papaya Paste: Choosing the correct papaya is very important as best paste can be made from baby papayas with the skin. Puree it to get a smooth paste. For best results, use a traditional stone grinder and feel the slimy texture in your fingers. However, pastes done in mixer grinders can also be used if the purpose is common, to tenderise the meat.

Khus Khus Paste: Especially used by experts, it is generally used in limited quantity with kebab marination and curries. The poppy seeds are used to make a fine paste.

Gram Flour Roux: It is a thickening mixture made with equal parts of gram flour (*besan*) and fat (*ghee*). It gives a pleasant nutty flavour to the dish and also brings all the flavours of the dish together.

MARINADES

A good marination is always recommended while cooking various types of meats. The first kind is done using a ginger garlic paste while the other one can be using any malt vinegar or lemon juice with a nice seasoning.

Tip: During my training days, while prepping marinades, I learnt that it is always good to keep the seasoning and spice level on a higher side to get the best taste in the final dish as most of it is macerated and absorbed in the main dish. I am listing below some of our basic recipes for a good marination. This makes for an approximate 1 kg marinade. An alternative to Kashmiri chilli powder is that you can prepare a paste by grinding de-seeded soaked chilli.

Red Marinade
Ingredients
Thick hung yoghurt or Greek yoghurt – 900 g
Ginger garlic paste – 4 tbsp
Kashmiri chilli powder – 3 tbsp
Turmeric powder – ½ tsp
Lemon juice – 2 tbsp
Garam masala – 1 tbsp
Mace powder – 1 tsp
Cardamom powder – 2 tsp
Cumin powder – 1 tsp
Vegetable oil – 80 ml
Salt to taste

Method
Mix all the ingredients in a bowl and whisk until the mixture becomes smooth. Check for lumps or whisk again.

Yellow Marinade

Ingredients

Thick hung yoghurt or Greek yoghurt – 900 g
Ginger garlic paste – 4 tbsp
Turmeric powder – 2 tsp
Yellow chilli powder – 2 tbsp
Lemon juice – 2 no
Garam masala – 1 tbsp
Mace powder – 1 tsp
Cardamom powder – 2 tsp
Cumin powder – 1 tsp
Vegetable oil – 80 ml
Salt to taste

Method

Mix all the ingredients in a bowl and whisk to a smooth paste with no lump formation. Don't be disappointed if you don't see yellow colour immediately after mixing, as turmeric always leaves it colour only after a while.

White Marinade

Ingredients

Thick hung yoghurt or Greek yoghurt – 400 g
Ginger garlic paste – 4 tbsp
Processed Amul cheese or mascarpone cheese – 200 g
Green chilli finely chopped – 2 tbsp
Single cream – 200 ml
Vegetable oil – 50 ml
Cardamom powder – 1 tsp
Coriander roots chopped – 3 tbsp
Salt to taste

Method

Mix all the ingredients in a bowl and whisk to prepare a smooth paste with no lumps.

Modern Indian Vegetarian Cuisine

GRAVIES AND SAUCES

Technically we should call all bases as sauces, however in Indian cuisine we commonly refer to them as gravy. Here are few basic recipes for gravies that make the foundation for all sauces.

Tip: It is very important to ensure all the ingredients are cooked properly as this helps in getting the desired shelf life and it is also vital from food safety perspective.

Makhni Sauce

This is one of the basic sauces of the Indian cuisine. Its vibrance is complemented by the earthy spices and herbs which is further mellowed with cream.

Ingredients

Oil – 2 tbsp
Cashew nut pieces – 80 g
Ginger paste – 1 tbsp
Garlic paste – 1 tbsp
Tomatoes roughly cut – 500 g
Tomato puree – 100 g
Kashmiri chilli powder – ½ tsp
Cumin powder – ½ tsp
Coriander roots – 4 g
Green Cardamom whole – 3 no
Butter – 50 g
Cooking cream – 60 g
Honey – 2 tbsp
Kasuri methi powder – ½ tsp
Garam masala – ½ tsp
Salt to taste

Method

Heat oil in a pan, add ginger garlic paste; as it is being cooked, stir in cashew nut pieces and lightly sauté until light golden.

Add the tomatoes and season, stir in slowly the tomato puree, sauté a little and then add water, cardamom pods and powdered spices. Again, add a little water and coriander roots. Simmer until the tomatoes are cooked and all the flavours from whole spices and herbs have infused.

Once the sauce is cooked, cool it down and blend the mixture in a fine blender until very smooth. Strain the mixture through a chinois or a strainer and ensure that you press the chinois to extract maximum juice with minimum waste.

Place the sauce again on heat and to balance the sourness of tomatoes add honey. Then add cream, butter, kasuri methi powder and finally finish with garam masala.

Onion Tomato Masala

One of the basic sauces of Indian cuisine is made in almost every Indian household.

Ingredients

Oil – 3 tbsp
Cumin whole – ½ tsp
Onion chopped – 220 g
Ginger chopped – 1 tbsp
Garlic chopped – 1 tbsp
Green chilli chopped – 2 no
Tomato puree – 100 g
Tomato fresh chopped – 200 g
Turmeric powder – ¼ tsp
Red chilli powder – ¼ tsp
Coriander powder – ½ tsp
Cumin powder – ½ tsp
Garam masala – ½ tsp
Salt to taste

Method

Heat oil in a pan, then add cumin seeds; once they begin to crackle, add chopped onion and cook till golden.

Add chopped ginger garlic, green chilli then the tomato paste and tomato puree. Stir in the powdered spices while adding a little water. Cook these until oil begins to separate on the sides and tomatoes are cooked.

Season and finish by adding garam masala.

Indian Brown Sauce/Gravy

It is an Indian sauce made with nuts and has a versatile use in various recipes.

Ingredients

Vegetable oil – ½ cup
Ginger paste – 2 tbsp
Garlic paste – 3 tbsp

Yoghurt smoothly whisked – 300 g
Tomato puree – 350 g
Coriander powder – 1 tbsp
Kashmiri chilli powder – 1 tsp
Cumin powder – 1 tsp
Fried onion paste – 50 g
Fried cashew nut paste – 50 g
Fried charoli or chironji nut paste – 50 g
Fried almonds paste – 50 g
Cardamom powder – ½ tsp
Garam masala powder – ½ tsp
Salt to taste

Method

Heat vegetable oil in a pan, add ginger garlic paste and stir until it is sautéed. Add yoghurt and cook while ensuring that it does not get curdled. Or you may use full cream yoghurt as well.

Add the tomato puree and cook until oil separates, then add the spices, except cardamon and garam masala, diluting it with little water.

Then start by adding the onion paste and nuts paste.

Season and add little water to ensure the sauce does not burn. Cover the pot as you keep it on flame.

Keep stirring in between until the oil fully separates on the sides and the sauce is cooked.

Sprinkle some garam masala and cardamom powder to the sauce to finish it off.

White Sauce/Gravy

This sauce is predominately known as shahi sauce or a spicy creamy sauce with green chillies.

Ingredients for Paste

Red onions – 400 g
Green chillies – 2 no
Green cardamom whole – 4 no
Bay leaf – 1 no
Broken cashew nuts – 400 g

Tempering
Vegetable oil – ½ cup
Ginger paste – 1 tbsp
Garlic paste – 1 tbsp
Yoghurt full cream – 150 g
White pepper to taste
Salt to taste

Method

Boil the onions, green chilli, cardamom, cashew nut and bay leaf in water until onions and cashew nut are completely soft.

Once the above mixture is cooked, cool it down and remove the bay leaf from it.

Grind the sauce to make a smooth paste.

Heat some oil in a pan, add ginger garlic paste and then add the whisked full cream yoghurt. Once it is cooked, add the onion mix paste and continuously stir until the sauce comes to boil.

After it boils, keep cooking while occasionally stirring until the oil separates and forms a layer on top.

Season the gravy and use as desired in any dish.

Dips and Chutneys

Beetroot Dip
Ingredients
Fresh beetroot juice – 50 g
Thick yoghurt – 400 g
Eggless mayonnaise – 100 g
Salt to taste
Pepper to taste

Method

Blend all the ingredients to prepare a smooth pouring consistency. Use it as a dip or as a garnish.

Tomato Chutney

Ingredients

Ripe tomatoes chopped – 500 g
Vegetable oil – 2 tbsp
Fennel seeds – ½ tsp
Mustard seeds – ¼ tsp
Cumin seeds – ½ tsp
Curry leaves – 5-6 no
Chopped onion – 40 g
Chopped garlic – 1 tbsp
Chopped ginger – 1 tbsp
Kashmiri chilli powder – 1 tbsp
Cardamom powder – ½ tsp
Sugar – 30 g
Salt to taste

Method

Heat oil in a pan, then add fennel, cumin and mustard seeds. As they begin to crackle, stir in curry leaves, onions and cook until it turns translucent. Add chopped garlic, ginger and cook until both garlic and ginger are properly cooked.

Add tomatoes and Kashmiri chilli powder in the mix, season with sugar and salt and cook until oil separates.

Once the oil separates and tomatoes are cooked, finish it off with cardamom powder.

This chutney can be served both as coarse or a smooth paste. You may even blend it to make a fine paste to store in a squeezy bottle and adjust its consistency if so required.

Saffron Dip

Ingredients

Saffron strands – 5-6 no
Thick hung yoghurt – 200 g
Eggless mayonnaise – 100 g
Salt and pepper to taste

Method

Dry roast the saffron on low heat (broil) and then pound it in mortar and pestle while adding little water to ensure it is fully blended.

Blend in rest of the ingredients with the saffron paste until you get smooth pouring consistency.

This can be used for garnish or as a dip.

Herb Coriander Dip

We have been making mint chutney since ages to be served with kebabs which only compliment the dish when it comes to taste. I am sharing a recipe that will have a similar taste but with a more eye appealing refreshing green colour. Here is my take on mint coriander chutney, made in the same way as pesto.

Ingredients

Coriander leaves – 200 g

Mint leaves – 10 g

Garlic cloves – 2 no

Green chilli deseeded – 2 no

Chaat masala – 1 tsp

Oil – ½ cup

Lemon juice – 1 tbsp

Salt to taste

Method

Wash the mint leaves in cold water and drain.

Quick blanch the coriander leaves in hot boiling water (not more than 5 seconds in hot water) and immediately chill these in ice water.

Spread the coriander leaves on baking trays and dehydrate the excess water in low heat in the oven at 20 degrees C for 2 hrs.

Keep the blender jar in freezer for 2 hrs before blending as it helps to retain the green colour.

Blend fresh mint, dehydrated coriander, oil, garlic, green chilli, chaat masala and lemon juice all together in the chilled jar and season to taste.

SPICES AND HERBS

Herbs and spices enhance flavour of the food and they also have medicinal and nutritional properties. Herbs are the aromatic leaves of fresh or dried plants whereas spices are the aromatic parts of plants that thrive in the tropical region. They are usually in the form of dried buds, fruits, berries, roots or barks.

In Indian cuisine it is very important to use the spices in correct sequence while understanding their basic composition. They form a solid foundation for any recipe. In this book, I have kept the use of spices to a minimum as they should not overpower the natural flavour of the vegetables. These should blend in smoothly as the final dish comes together.

I have simply mystified the repertoire here.

Tempering Spices

Cumin whole, mustard seeds, fenugreek seeds, onion seeds, whole spices, ajwain seeds, coriander seeds, fennel – all these spices release their flavour as they crackle and are cooked in a heavy bottomed pan. One has to master the art of right time to add the other ingredients and not burn the dish.

Thickeners and Flavouring

All the spices used should be broiled (dry roasted) and powdered coarsely or a fine residue depending on the dish; examples of these are turmeric powder, chilli powder and coriander powder.

Turmeric: I personally prefer grinding my own turmeric powder as commercial ones have synthetic colours and never impart the natural golden yellow colour. Cooking of turmeric is an art; I prefer to cook it just right as this spice is fastest to cook when you add it for tempering. It releases its colour almost after 24 hours into marination.

Chilli: There are many varieties of chilli powders available in the market from degi mirch, Andhra style to Kashmiri chilli powder. I prefer to make my dishes by using the Kashmiri chillies as these impart a very nice colour without making the dish too hot.

Coriander: One of my favourite powders as it thickens the dish and brings it together. In all its forms, powder, coarse or as a whole, it adds texture and flavour to the dish.

Asafoetida: This comes from resin of a tree and is very important in vegetarian cuisine. I always feel it acts like a catalyst, as it brings the dish together with its subtle flavour. It is also very good for digestion of food.

Cumin: I prefer to add this at a later stage in the dish as it turns the dish a bit dark and loses its flavour. Adding this spice is purely a personal choice.

Aromatic Spices

Fennel, cardamom, saffron, rose powder, sandalwood powder, stone flower and garam masala powder all impart a nice flavour to the dish and each one has a very distinctive aroma. All the spices should be used in moderation and usually at the end of finishing the dish so as to retain maximum flavour.

My special spice mix is curry powder.

Curry powder: I always felt we should have a separate spice mix, as in India, we have these individual spices grounded separately. When I travelled abroad and worked with international chefs, I realised that curry powder is very important as it helps to make the curry easier, simpler and consistent. Below is my own recipe for this special curry powder.

Ingredients to prepare 1 kg

Coriander seeds whole – 400 g

Cumin seeds whole – 200 g

Fennel seeds – 100 g

Black pepper whole – 30 g

Turmeric powder – 100 g

Chilli whole red dried – 20 g

Garlic powder – 100 g

Ginger powder – 50 g

Method

Separately broil/toast the whole seeds and keep aside to cool.

Grind one by one all the ingredients to get the powdered form.

Mix all the grinded ingredients along with powdered ingredients to get a fine texture.

Garam Masala

A very important part of Indian cooking as it enhances and aromatises the dish. It should always be added at the end to get maximum flavours.

Ingredients

Green cardamom – 100 g
Black cardamom seeds – 40 g
Clove – 5 g
Cinnamon – 180 g
Nutmeg – 5 g
Mace – 15 g
Dry rose petal – 100 g
Dry ginger – 80 g
Black pepper – 30 g
Cumin seeds – 300 g
Coriander seeds – 150 g
Bay leaf – 5-6 no
Shahi jeera (black cumin seeds) – 100 g

Method

Broil all the spices on slow heat. Cool the spices and blend into fine powder in a blender and strain the spice mix through muslin.

Chettinad Masala

Ingredients

Cloves whole – 5 g
Cinnamon whole – 200 g
Fennel – 50 g
Cumin seeds whole – 200 g
Star anise – 50 g
Black pepper whole – 30 g
Cardamom green – 200 g
Mace – 20 g
Bay leaves – 8-9 no

Black stone flower – 20 g

Coriander seeds – 200 g

Method

Broil all the spices on slow heat. Cool the spices and blend into fine powder in a blender and strain the spice mix through muslin.

Tip: Store it in a sanitised dry glass jar. Cover well. Make in small quantities, fresh is always better.

PICKLES

Pickled-style recipes in India vary from one region to the other. I have listed two of my favourite recipes, however these may be altered based on personal choice and experience.

Tips to handle pickles

Never use wet hands/spoons while transferring pickles into small containers, as moisture leads to fungal growth.

Always use a clean dry spoon for taking out pickles from the jar.

Close the jar immediately to prevent fungus spores from falling in. These are present in the atmosphere specially during rainy season.

Always cover the vegetables with oil or vinegar as it can develop fungus on the top layer.

Green Chillies Pickle

Ingredients

Green chillies chopped – 500 g	Salt – 80 g	Cumin seed – 2 tbsp
Garlic paste – 80 g	Sugar – 30 g	White vinegar – 1.5 cup
Ginger paste – 80 g	Turmeric powder – 2 tbsp	Mustard oil – 1.5 cup

Method

Choose ripe, fresh green chillies; wash them and then pat them dry completely.

Finely chop the green chillies and set them aside.

Mix ginger and garlic paste, turmeric, salt and sugar in another bowl.

Heat the mustard oil to smoking point and then let it cool to moderate cooking temperature to mellow its pungency; then add cumin seeds, as they crackle, stir in the mix prepared; cook on low heat; add chopped green chillies and season with salt and sugar; keep cooking until oil comes on top.

Add vinegar and cool the mixture; store in an airtight jar.

Mango Pickle

Ingredients

Raw mango – 2 kg
Mustard seeds – 2 tbsp
Fennel seeds – 2 tbsp
Fenugreek seeds – 1 tbsp

Ajwain seeds – ½ tbsp
Kashmiri chilli powder – 3 tbsp
Turmeric powder – 2 tbsp
Cumin powder – 1 tbsp

Mustard oil – 1 lt
Salt – 100 g
Black salt – 50 g
Asafoetida (hing) – ½ g

Method

Cut raw mango with seed to equal size and remove any excess moisture. Mix in salt and hing.

Let it dry in sun for three days.

Mix all the spices, seeds and mustard oil with the mangoes (***Tip:*** the oil should be heated to smoking point and cooled to mellow down its pungency).

Cover the pot and ensure it is kept in the sun for fifteen days; stir every day to mix in the spices with a clean dry spoon.

Serve after fifteen days; store in an airtight jar.

STARTERS

Palak Anjeer Kebab 02
Teekhe Matar and Oats Kebab 04
Dahi Kebab 07
Tulsi Paneer Tikka 08
Doodhiya Kebab 10
Makai Paneer Gilori 13
Besan Ke Sikke 14
Khichdi Arancini 16
Mirchi Kebab 18

PALAK ANJEER KEBAB
(Fig and Spinach Kebab)

I learned this dish while making the original dish Hara Kebab when I was working with master chefs in India, 2006. The principle is the same, however I added my twist by adding sweetness and crunch from cashew nuts and dried fig. The dish is not overly spiced to ensure that each ingredient retains its taste. I recommend to serve this dish with any chutney of your choice. A great way to begin the meal and tickle your palate.

Serves 4

INGREDIENTS

Vegetable oil – 2 tbsp

Ginger paste – 1 tbsp

Garlic paste – 1 tbsp

Spinach leaves blanched and pureed – 300 g

Channa dal (lentil) raw – 1/3 cup

Green chilli finely chopped – 1 tsp

Kasuri methi dried and powdered – ¼ tsp

Salt to taste

STUFFING

Dry fig soaked and chopped – 80 g

Grated cheddar cheese – 3 tbsp

Chopped green chillies – ¼ tsp

Cashew nuts fried crushed – 2 tbsp

Coriander roots chopped – 3 g

Salt to taste

FOR PAN GRILL

Vegetable oil or ghee – 2 tbsp

METHOD

Dal (Lentil) Paste

Wash and soak the dal for a minimum of 2 hrs before cooking the dish.

Place the chana dal in a pot, add salt and cover with water, simmer until it is completely cooked (pressure cooker can be used to save time). Drain excess water and keep aside the dal for cooling.

Once it is cold, grind the dal to a fine paste and cook on low heat in a heavy bottomed pan while stirring continuously until it becomes dry.

Heat oil in a pan, add ginger garlic paste, sauté a little until raw flavour is evaporated.

Add the dry lentil paste and reduce the heat, stir continuously until cooked. Now fold in the thick pureed spinach and season, add green chilli. Cook until thick mixture is formed, then finally add kasuri methi powder. Leave the mixture for cooling.

STUFFING

Prepare the stuffing by mixing all the ingredients together.

Take the mixture in hand and divide it into equal size to make small tight 30 g balls.

(Tip: Always rest the shaped patty in refrigerator for 2 hrs before grilling as it helps to retain shape and texture.)

KEBABS

Prepare a kebab using the spinach lentil mixture and then make a hole in the centre. Fill the stuffing inside and then roll into flattened discs.

Pan grill the kebab on non-stick pan or griddle on each side and serve hot.

Carbs	Fat	Protein	Fiber	Sugar	Sodium
15.25 gms	21.5 gms	6.75 gms	5 gms	5 gms	243.75 mg

Per serving

Calories per seving: 288.75 kcal

TEEKHE MATAR AND OATS KEBAB
(Spicy Oats and Green Pea Kebab)

When I served kebabs in Dubai, one of my customers called me and gave me constructive feedback. He said, "I always felt heavy after having Indian food as the menu usually did not offer any healthy options." It inspired me to create this dish in 2011 Sheraton Dubai for the Aashiana Restaurant which became a hot selling and quite a popular dish. An oats and green pea patty crusted with wheat husk (a technique I learnt from a chef in ITC which really makes the kebab crispy). Oats can be used as a binding ingredient, therefore it is not always true that one needs a starch or a heavy protein to bind the them together.

Vegan/Serves 4

INGREDIENTS

Vegetable oil – 1.5 tbsp

Cumin seeds – ¼ tsp

Onions chopped – 2 tbsp

Garlic finely chopped – 1 tbsp

Ginger finely chopped – 1 tbsp

Green chilli chopped – 1 tsp

Baby green peas – 200 g

Oats dry – 70 g (to be soaked in water)

Mint leaves chopped – 3 g

Garam masala – ¼ tsp

TO CRUMB

Flour slurry (combine refined flour and water to make a thin slurry)

Wheat husk (isabgol) for crumbing

Olive oil for pan fry

Chaat masala – 1tsp

METHOD

Heat oil in a pan, add cumin seeds, once it starts crackling and changing colour, stir in the chopped onions.

Cook the onions until translucent, then add garlic, ginger and green chillies, sauté the mix lightly.

Stir in the green peas and season, lightly mash the green peas with back of the spoon and add the soaked and squeezed mixture of oats; mix together. Finish with garam masala and keep the mixture for cooling; once it is cold, mix the chopped mint to get the fresh flavour from it. *(Tip: I recommend this as it gets best flavours from the herbs without losing colour).*

Shape the kebab into a patty or a disc and prepare the slurry for crumbing by mixing refined flour and water.

Dip the kebab in slurry and then in wheat husk and pan fry in olive oil. *(Tip: always rest the shaped patty in refrigerator for 2 hrs before grilling it as helps to retain its shape and texture.)*

Sprinkle chaat masala on the patty before serving.

Per serving

Calories per seving: 312.25 kcal

Carbs	Fat	Protein	Fiber	Sugar	Sodium
18.25 gms	9.25 gms	3.75 gms	6 gms	2.75 gms	118.25 mg

DAHI KEBAB
(Yoghurt Kebab)

Yoghurt kebab was very common on menus in banquets during 2008-2009. I still remember whenever it comes to high volumes, my chefs always wanted to make deep fried version of kebab as it was easier to manage. It was hard to convince them to do pan grill kebabs as it was time consuming and labour intensive but definitely better. I have added my twist to the kebab by adding a different type of stuffing. It is mouth melting; the pickled stuffing has succulent flavours that just burst in your mouth which can kick start a jaded palate.

Serves 4

INGREDIENTS

Dough

Chenna or freshly made cottage cheese – 330 g

White pepper – ½ tsp

Roasted cumin powder – 1 tsp

Roasted channa powder – 2 tbsp

Chaat masala – 1 tsp

Fresh coriander leave finely chopped – 1 tsp

STUFFING

Greek or hung yoghurt – 100 g

Grated processed cheese – 30 g

Chopped ginger – 1 tsp

Green chillies deseeded chopped – ½ tsp

Pickle paste (mango pickle blended without the core) – 2 tbsp

Coriander roots chopped – 1 tsp

Chaat masala – 1 tsp

Salt to taste

Oil to pan grill

METHOD

Make a dough for kebabs with all the ingredients by rubbing with hands and adding the spices. Make sure there are no lumps in the mixture.

Prepare the stuffing with all the ingredients by mixing them together.

Take the dough mixtures and divide it into equal size portions around 20 g each. Make hole in the centre and fill with stuffing and then roll into discs. Rest the patty in the fridge for at least 2-3 hrs as this helps in holding the shape.

Pan grill the kebab on both sides using oil on griddle or non-stick pan and serve with chutney.

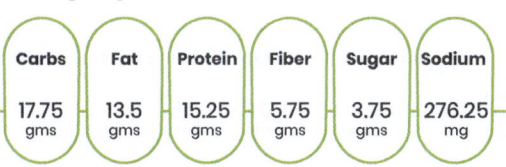

Carbs	Fat	Protein	Fiber	Sugar	Sodium
17.75 gms	13.5 gms	15.25 gms	5.75 gms	3.75 gms	276.25 mg

Per serving

Calories per seving: 174.75 kcal

TULSI PANEER TIKKA
(Cottage Cheese and Basil Kebab)

Sweet basil is an excellent herb and is commonly used in western cuisine as it has a range of benefits. While making the green chutney, I wanted to use basil in the marinade and thought it would combine best with paneer which has a neutral flavour and absorbs the marinade quite nicely. Basil and spicy yoghurt marinate combines well with paneer and finally the smoky tandoor cooking with glaze of olive oil add a delectable taste.

Serves 4

INGREDIENTS

Cottage cheese cut into 2-inch cubes – 500 g

Greek yoghurt or hung curd – 100 g

PASTE

Ginger paste – 1 tbsp

Garlic paste – 1 tbsp

Green chillies – 1-2 no

Basil leaves – 30 g

Coriander leaves – 10 g

Chaat masala – 1 tbsp

Garam masala – 1 tsp

Extra virgin olive oil – 40 g

Salt to taste

TO SPRINKLE

Chaat masala – 10 g

Extra virgin olive oil – 10 g

METHOD

Make a marinade by blending all the ingredients of the paste, mix the Greek yoghurt with the paste to thicken it. *(Tip: always season the marinade with spices and it should be strong as it mellows when absorbed by the protein and brings best taste of the dish.)*

Marinate the paneer for minimum 4-5 hrs.

Grill in moderately heated clay oven (tandoor) and baste occasionally with olive oil.

Finish with a sprinkling of chaat masala and olive oil.

Per serving

Calories per seving: 575.75 kcal

Carbs	Fat	Protein	Fiber	Sugar	Sodium
10.75 gms	17.25 gms	15 gms	1 gms	6.5 gms	16.5 mg

DOODHIYA KEBAB
(Stuffed Cottage Cheese Kebab)

I learned and developed this recipe while working with ITC Hotels with one of the master chefs. I saw the use of wheat husk/Isabgol. I always thought that it is used as medicine for digestive reasons, however after reading it contents, I realised it is just natural wheat and when I tasted the kebab after frying, it was very crispy and stable. This recipe is one of my personal favourites as sweet and sour potatoes really combine well with marinated paneer and the crumby texture adds to the taste of kebab, a delight to eat.

Serves 4

INGREDIENTS
Paneer or cottage cheese whole block – 600 g

MARINADE
White pepper powder – 1 tsp
Chaat masala – 1 tsp
Lemon juice – 1.5 tbsp
Yellow chilli powder – ½ tsp

STUFFING
Vegetable oil – 2 tbsp
Shahi jeera or black cumin – 1 tsp
Chopped onions – 50 g
Kashmiri chilli powder – 1 tsp
Tomato ketchup – 2 tbsp
Grated potatoes – 300 g
Chopped ginger – 1 tbsp
Cumin powder – ½ tsp
Amchur powder – 1 tsp
Garam masala – ½ tsp
Chopped coriander leaves – 1 tbsp
Salt to taste

FOR CRUMBING
Refined flour slurry
Psyllium husk/Isabgol or breadcrumbs panko – 200 g
Vegetable oil or ghee to pan grill – 2 tbsp

METHOD

Heat the oil in a pan, then add black cumin and sauté lightly.

Add finely chopped onions, sauté until pink in colour, stir in ginger, chilli powder and ketchup, then stir in the grated potatoes, salt, amchur powder, cumin powder and garam masala. Add chopped coriander when the mixture is cold.

Cut the paneer into very thin slices to desired shapes – squares or roundels (approximately 1 cm size).

Marinate paneer for minimum 2-3 hrs to absorb the flavours and spices.

Sandwich the paneer with the above mixture and set aside. Prepare refined flour and water slurry of thin consistency.

Use the psyllium husks to crumb.

Carefully dip the paneer in slurry and then crumbs and refrigerate for at least 2 hrs.

Pan grill the kebabs until crisp and golden colour.

Serve with chutney

Note: Left over trimmings from paneer can be used in salads or stuffing of your choice.

Carbs	Fat	Protein	Fiber	Sugar	Sodium
22 gms	51 gms	34.75 gms	3 gms	3.5 gms	188.5 mg

Per serving

Calories per seving: 229 kcal

MAKAI PANEER GILORI
(Corn and Cottage Cheese Triangular Rolls)

This dish is inspired from famous ginger Gilori pickle from old Delhi, studded with a clove, which prevents it from opening. The shape of the pickle gave me an idea to name this dish and instead of ginger I have used triangular spring roll sheets filled with spicy tender corn and paneer served with beetroot chutney.

Serves 4

INGREDIENTS

Vegetable oil – 2 tbsp

Shahi jeera/black cumin – 1 tsp

Onion chopped – 50 g

Ginger chopped – 1 tbsp

Garlic chopped – 1 tbsp

Corn kernels crushed coarsely – 200 g

Green chilli chopped – 1 tsp

Cottage cheese or paneer grated – 400 g

Garam masala – ½ tsp

Chaat masala – 1 tsp

Cardamom powder – ½ tsp

Fennel powder – ½ tsp

Spring roll pastry sheets 4 cm x 4 cm – 1 pkt

Flour slurry (combine refined flour and water to make thin slurry)

Salt to taste

METHOD

Heat oil in a pan, add shahi jeera and as it crackles add the chopped onion and season; cook until onions turn pink, stir in the ginger and garlic, add corn kernels coarsely crushed and sauté. Add chopped green chillies and grated cottage cheese mixture.

Spice with garam masala, cardamom and fennel powder and finally add chaat masala.

Remove the mixture from the burner and leave it for cooling.

Cut the spring roll pastry into squares and place the mixture in the centre and prepare it in triangular shape.

Seal the pastry with refined flour slurry and bake in a preheated oven for 10 min at 180 degrees centigrade until golden colour.

Carbs	Fat	Protein	Fiber	Sugar	Sodium
33.75 gms	38.25 gms	28.5 gms	4.75 gms	4.75 gms	231 mg

Per serving

Calories per seving: 511 kcal

BESAN KE SIKKE
(Spicy Gram Flour Coins)

This kebab dish is inspired from a Rajasthani main course dish called pithod, since it is very similar to the original dish, as the technique used to make both are similar and it is a delight for vegetarians. If you do not take garlic or ginger it can be substituted with hing or asafoetida.

Serves 4

INGREDIENTS

BATTER

Besan – 1 cup
Turmeric powder – ½ tsp
Ajwain or carom seeds – ½ tsp
Red chilli powder – 1 tsp
Ginger paste – 1 tbsp
Garlic paste – 1 tbsp
Butter milk – 1 cup
Vegetable oil – 1/3 cup
Water – 2 cups
Salt to taste

SPRINKLE

Grated processed cheese – 60 g
Coriander chopped – 2 g
Vegetable oil for greasing the tray – 1 tsp

PAN GRILL

Vegetable oil – 3 tbsp

METHOD

Make a batter using all the ingredients; ensure there are no lumps, and the mixture is smooth (add water slowly to the flour to avoid lumps and whisk the mixture continuously).

Once the batter is ready, pour it in a heavy bottomed pan.

Cook slowly on low heat and continue stirring until it starts to leave the sides of the pan and is of thick consistency.

Prepare a greased tray and pour the batter on it after removing from heat and spread it evenly using a palate knife to ensure that the surface is smooth and levelled.

Sprinkle cheese and coriander on the hot tray and leave it for cooling.

Once cooled, cut into round shape with the help of mould of size of a coin.

Lightly pan grill in oil before serving.

Note: Left over trimmings from besan may be used in gravies or sauces.

Per serving
Calories per seving: 382.5 kcal

Carbs	Fat	Protein	Fiber	Sugar	Sodium
36.25 gms	25.75 gms	13.5 gms	3.75 gms	4.75 gms	371.5 mg

KHICHDI ARANCINI
(Lentil Rice and Crispy Vegetable Dumplings)

I always believed that our traditional khichdi is an amazing complete meal as it has protein starch and vegetables in correct quantity. There is saying in India – khichdi tere chaar yaar, ghee, papad, dahi, te achar (khichdi you have four friends – ghee, papad, curd and pickle). Tasty and well-prepared khichdi can be a nice meal altogether. I was inspired to create this experience in grazing portions with a contemporary presentation.

Serves 4

INGREDIENTS

Basmati rice – 1 cup
Yellow moong dal – ½ cup
Vegetable oil – 4 tbsp
Cumin seeds – 1 tsp
Onion seeds – ¼ tsp
Fennel seeds – ½ tsp
Carom seeds – ¼ tsp
Red onion chopped – 80 g
Chopped ginger – 1 tbsp
Chopped garlic – 1 tbsp
Green chilli chopped – ½ tbsp
Turmeric powder – 1 tsp
Coriander powder – 1 tsp
Red chilli powder – ½ tsp
Coriander leaves chopped – 1 g
Water – 450 ml
Ghee – 1 tbsp

STUFFING

Hung curd or Greek yoghurt – 60 g
Pickle mango pulp – 20 g

METHOD

Wash the rice and dal and soak for 15-20 mins.

Heat oil in a pan, add cumin seeds, onion seeds, fennel seeds and carom seeds; as soon as it begins to crackles, add chopped onions and cook until light golden. Then add chopped ginger, garlic and green chillies; cook until garlic is cooked, stir in the soaked rice, dal and powdered spices.

Add water, season and stir in the ghee; cover the pot and cook until rice and lentil is overcooked for 15-20 mins. Cool the rice khichdi; then add the chopped coriander.

STUFFING

Prepare the stuffing with Greek or hung curd, pickle paste, chopped ginger, coriander and grated cheese.

Take the cold khichdi portion and stuff with the pickled mixture and shape into equal sized balls, about 25 g each.

	Carbs	Fat	Protein	Fiber	Sugar	Sodium
Per serving	31 gms	22.5 gms	7 gms	3 gms	2.5 gms	181.5 mg

Calories per seving: 429.75 kcal

Ginger chopped – 1 tsp
Green chilli chopped – 1 g
Coriander leaves chopped – 1 tsp
Grated cheese – 40 g

FOR CRUMBING

Flour slurry (combine refined flour and water to make thin slurry)
Panko crumbs to crust
Vegetable oil to deep fry

CRUMBING

Make the slurry of refined flour and dip each ball of khichdi and crust with panko.

Continue the same process for rest of the khichdi and chill the stuffed balls for an hour as it helps to retain its shape before frying.

Deep fry the arancini balls and serve hot.

Modern Indian Vegetarian Cuisine

MIRCHI KEBAB
(Stuffed Chilli Kebab)

Fresh chillies or peppers always inspire me to use them owing to their colour, pungency and flavour. The art in this kebab is to keep the chilli crisp and right texture with burst of flavours combining in the mouth. I made this dish in the Middle East where you can get produce from all over the world. If you don't get different colours use green large chillies which are readily available. I have stuffed them with a potato cheese mixture and grilled to perfection.

Serves 4

INGREDIENTS

Green chilli large – 2 no
Red chilli large – 2 no
Yellow chilli large – 2 no
Orange chilli large – 2 no

MARINADE FOR CHILLIES

Olive oil – 2 tbsp
Chaat masala – 1 tsp
Salt to taste

STUFFING

Vegetable oil – 2 tbsp
Cumin seeds – ½ tsp
Onions chopped – 40 g
Ginger chopped – 1 tbsp
Garlic chopped – ½ tbsp
Potato grated boiled – 200 g
Chaat masala – 1 tbsp
Paneer – 100 g
Green chilli chopped – 1 tsp
Fennel seeds toasted and crushed – 1 tsp
Grated cheddar cheese – 50 g
Coriander chopped – 2 g
Vegetable oil to grill

METHOD

Wash the chillies and slit them in the centre, deseed them and marinate with olive oil, chaat masala and salt; ensure it is rubbed evenly all around and inside as well. Leave for 3 to 4 hrs.

Prepare the stuffing by heating vegetable oil, add cumin seeds and as they splutter, stir in the onions; as they become translucent, add ginger and garlic; sauté a little until garlic is cooked.

Add the grated potato, paneer, green chilli and sprinkle the spice powders and fennel seeds powder for aroma.

Finish with grated cheese and add coriander when the mixture is cold to retain colour and flavour.

Stuff the chillies with the mixture and set aside for 2-3 hrs. Lightly grill on high heat or until you see the grill marks on the chillies.

Serve with chutney.

Per serving
Calories per seving: 394.5 kcal

Carbs	Fat	Protein	Fiber	Sugar	Sodium
22 gms	30.5 gms	12.25 gms	3 gms	2.5 gms	120.5 mg

SALADS

Moong Sprouts, Broken Wheat, Cucumber, Bell Pepper, Toasted Almond Salad 22

Deconstructed Mango Peanut Kachumber 24

Burrani Palak 27

Chickpeas, Corn, Cucumber and Walnut Salad 29

Nimki 30

Heirloom Tomatoes, Fresh Paneer and Coriander Chutney Salad 33

Roasted Pumpkin, Cherry Tomato and Fresh Chenna Salad 34

Lentil Salad with Roasted Sweet Potato ... 37

Mooli Kanda 38

MOONG SPROUTS, BROKEN WHEAT, CUCUMBER, BELL PEPPER, TOASTED ALMOND SALAD

Sprouts are full of energy and broken wheat which we call daliya is quite healthy too. I have used all these ingredients to create a refreshing experience in your mouth with bite from almonds.

Serves 4

INGREDIENTS

Moong sprouts – 120 g
Broken wheat (dalia) – 150 g
Olive oil for boiling the broken wheat – ½ tsp
Lebanese Cucumber diced – 80 g
Bell pepper red diced – 80 g
Pomegranate seeds – 30 g

DRESSING

Extra virgin olive oil – 2 tbsp
Lemon juice – 2 tbsp
Salt to taste
Pepper to taste

GARNISH

Coriander sprigs – 3 g
Toasted almond flakes – 10 g

METHOD

Soak the broken wheat for minimum of 1 hr and cook in hot boiling water with little salt and drops of olive oil (this helps in keeping the grains separate and avoids it from sticking to each other) until cooked.

Strain the excess water and ensure there are no lumps. Cool the mixture down.

Make a smooth dressing with olive oil, lemon juice and seasoning.

Toss diced vegetables, sprouts, cooked broken wheat and dressing together just before serving and garnish with toasted almonds and coriander leaf.

Per serving
Calories per serving: 394.5 kcal

Carbs	Fat	Protein	Fiber	Sugar	Sodium
19.90 gms	12.79 gms	4.3 gms	5.47 gms	7.52 gms	69.2 mg

Salads

DECONSTRUCTED MANGO PEANUT KACHUMBER

Kachumber is the most famous and the most common salad in Indian food as it blends so well with all the dishes. I would like to showcase my take on kachumber using similar ingredients with an eye appealing appetising plating style.

Serves 4

INGREDIENTS

Carrots diced – 100 g
Cucumber diced – 120 g
Onions red diced – 40 g
Mango ripe diced – 150 g

DRESSING

Lemon juice – 1 tsp
Olive oil – ½ tbsp
Chopped coriander – 1 tsp
Chaat masala – 1 tsp
Salt to taste

PRESENTATION

Honey – 5 g for brushing
Roasted peanut crushed – 20 g
Cucumber shaved – 3 no
Carrot shaved – 2 no
Mango thick triangles – 20 g
Cherry tomato halves – 35 g
Baby raddish slices – 3 g
Mint sauce for plating
Beetroot yoghurt for plating
Micro herbs for garnish

METHOD

Make a dressing by gently whisking together olive oil, lemon juice and spices. Toss all the ingredients of the salad and dressing and keep aside.

PRESENTATION

Brush honey on the plate and then add roasted peanut, alternatively arrange cucumber, carrot and other garnishes on the plate and then place the kachumber salad between the rolls.

Garnish the salad with micro herbs.

Per serving
Calories per serving: 132.75 kcal

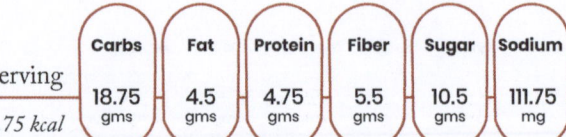

Carbs	Fat	Protein	Fiber	Sugar	Sodium
18.75 gms	4.5 gms	4.75 gms	5.5 gms	10.5 gms	111.75 mg

BURRANI PALAK
(Spinach with Garlic Yoghurt)

Burrani is a garlic flavoured yoghurt commonly served with Biryanis. This is a healthy spinach leaves salad with a hint of garlic and freshness from pomegranate seeds. I have used thick garlic flavoured yoghurt to make this salad a real energy booster that may be consumed anytime during the day.

Serves 4

INGREDIENTS
Baby spinach leaves – 250 g
Mint leaves chopped – 5-6 no
Sunflower seeds toasted – 10 g
Pomegranate seeds fresh – ¼ cup
Coriander leaves chopped – 5 g
Salt to taste

DRESSING
Black pepper crushed to taste
Hung/Greek yoghurt – 50 g
Garlic paste – ½ tsp
Extra virgin olive oil – 1 tsp
Micro herb for garnish

METHOD

Prepare the dressing with garlic, yoghurt, oil and salt by whisking together gently, then set aside.

Wash the spinach and mint leaves and ensure these are dried in a strainer or with a cloth before adding to the dressing.

Toss the dressing with spinach, coriander and mint leaves just before serving and top with sunflower and pomegranate seeds.

Drizzle little oil on top for glaze and garnish with micro herbs.

Carbs	Fat	Protein	Fiber	Sugar	Sodium
38.25 gms	5.5 gms	10.5 gms	10.5 gms	3.5 gms	46 mg

Per serving

Calories per serving: 280.5 kcal

Modern Indian Vegetarian Cuisine

CHICKPEAS, CORN, CUCUMBER AND WALNUT SALAD

It is a healthy combination of chickpea, vegetables and nuts which perfectly combines protein, fibre and nutty texture with a tinge of tangy chaat masala taste. The idea is to present the salad differently by layering it in a jar.

Serves 4

INGREDIENTS

Chickpeas boiled – 200 g

Corn kernels – 80 g

Toasted walnuts crushed – 20 g

Lebanese cucumber diced – 80 g

Baby spinach – 60 g

DRESSING

Olive oil – 2 tbsp

Chaat masala – 1 tsp

Lemon juice – ½ tsp

Salt to taste

Pepper to taste

GARNISH

Pomegranate seeds – 2 tbsp

METHOD

Make a smooth dressing with olive oil, chaat masala, lemon juice and seasoning.

Layer all the ingredients in the jar ensuring you have the right colour combinations and enough space to toss the ingredients in the jar before eating; pour the dressing on the salad or serve on the side.

Garnish with pomegranate seeds.

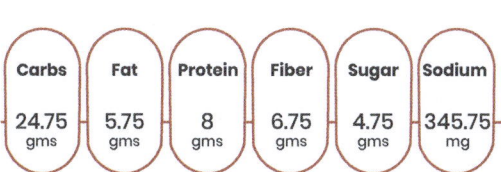

Per serving

Calories per seving: 205.5 kcal

Carbs	Fat	Protein	Fiber	Sugar	Sodium
24.75 gms	5.75 gms	8 gms	6.75 gms	4.75 gms	345.75 mg

NIMKI
(Raw Mango Salad)

I learnt this recipe from my family, especially while cooking with my mom in Shimla, as this is a delight in Himachal's Sood families. This dish is a very nice accompaniment to food and helps in providing a cooling sensation to the body and aids digestion.

Serves 4

INGREDIENTS
Raw mango peeled sliced thick – 400 g

Red onions sliced thick – 150 g

Ajwain seeds – 2 g

Lemon juice – 3 tbsp

Red chilli powder – ½ tsp

Sugar to taste

Salt to taste

FOR SMOKING
Charcoal – 1 no

Mustard oil – 1 tbsp

Cloves – 2 no

METHOD
Mix all the ingredients together in a deep bowl.

Place the salad in a deep dish in which you wish to serve, then make a bay in the centre to place the hot charcoal.

Heat the charcoal and put it in the centre of the bowl; pour mustard oil and cloves on the hot charcoal and cover the dish to ensure smoke gets inside the salad.

Serve after 15 mins once the smoky flavour has infused in the salad.

Per serving
Calories per serving: 85.75 kcal

Carbs	Fat	Protein	Fiber	Sugar	Sodium
35.25 gms	7 gms	2.5 gms	11.5 gms	17.25 gms	82 mg

Salads

Modern Indian Vegetarian Cuisine

HEIRLOOM TOMATOES, FRESH PANEER AND CORIANDER CHUTNEY SALAD

Fresh salad in Indian food confines to cucumber, radish, carrots or lentil, however this recipe came to my mind while eating an Italian caprese salad. The inspiration came from the colourful varieties of tomatoes available in the market combined with Indian-style freshly made paneer and drizzled with lush green and vibrant coriander chutney. Sometime, the simple, the better!

Serves 4

INGREDIENTS

Ripe heirloom tomatoes different colours – 8-9 no

Chenna/paneer freshly made – 150 g

Coriander chutney – 50 g

Salt to taste

Pepper to taste

Extra virgin olive oil – 1 tbsp

Micro herb for garnish

METHOD

Evenly cut the tomatoes into round slices approximately ½ cm thickness.

Season the chenna with salt and pepper.

Arrange the slices on the plate and place small quenelle on each slice neatly.

Drizzle the coriander chutney on the fresh chenna and garnish with micro herbs and oilve oil.

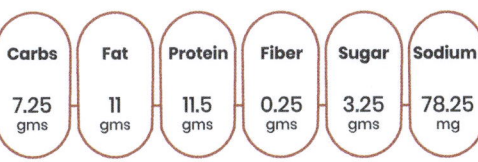

Per serving

Calories per seving: 283 kcal

Carbs	Fat	Protein	Fiber	Sugar	Sodium
7.25 gms	11 gms	11.5 gms	0.25 gms	3.25 gms	78.25 mg

ROASTED PUMPKIN, CHERRY TOMATO AND FRESH CHENNA SALAD

A good salad is refreshing, filling, colourful and healthy. I have used freshly made paneer to enrich the salad along with the crunch from toasted pumpkin seeds.

Serves 4

INGREDIENTS

Cherry tomato red cut in halves – 1 cup

Cherry tomato yellow cut in halves – 1 cup

Pumpkin triangles – 1 cup

Olive oil to brush the pumpkin

Beetroot wedges – 60 g

Coriander chutney – 2 tbsp

Toasted pumpkin seeds – 1 tbsp

Fresh chenna – 50 g

Salt to taste

METHOD

Put the pumpkin triangles on a hot grill until cooked and then season.

Place the beetroot wedges in cold water and season; then boil until the beetroot is cooked and drain the excess water.

Neatly arrange cherry tomatoes, cooked pumpkin, chenna dollops, beetroot and drizzle the coriander chutney to season and enhance the flavour.

Sprinkle toasted pumpkin seeds to add the crunchy texture.

Per serving

Calories per seving: 158 kcal

Carbs	Fat	Protein	Fiber	Sugar	Sodium
171 gms	11 gms	30 gms	15 gms	73.25 gms	48.5 mg

Salads

Modern Indian Vegetarian Cuisine

LENTIL SALAD WITH ROASTED SWEET POTATO

I was always inspired with the variety of street food available in Delhi. A plate of roasted sweet potato and dal moth used to sensuate my taste buds that had an amazing blend of spices and sour tamarind chutney with loads of freshly chopped coriander tossed together. Here is my take on the same chaat but with a modern presentation and a twist with similar flavours.

Serves 4

INGREDIENTS

Boiled brown lentils – 1.5 cup
Cumin powder – ¼ tsp
Chopped red onion – 1 tbsp
Raisins soaked – ½ tbsp
Sweet potato roasted peeled – 200 g
Chaat masala – ¼ tsp

DRESSING

Tamarind pulp – 2 tbsp
Olive oil – 1 tbsp
Pine nuts toasted – 1 tbsp
Lemon wedges – 4 slices
Salt to taste

METHOD

Gently whisk the tamarind pulp, olive oil and salt to make a dressing for the salad and set aside.

Toss the lentils, cumin powder, red onions and raisins with dressing to make a lentil salad mix.

Take the roasted peeled sweet potato and cut into wedges, sprinkle chaat masala. *(**Note:** Sweet potatoes can be roasted in charcoal fire or oven for 30-40 mins at 200 degrees C until the skin has puffed up.)*

Arrange sweet potato neatly on the lentil salad base, garnish along with lemon and toasted pine nuts.

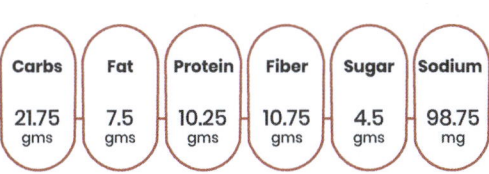

Carbs	Fat	Protein	Fiber	Sugar	Sodium
21.75 gms	7.5 gms	10.25 gms	10.75 gms	4.5 gms	98.75 mg

Per serving

Calories per seving: 144 kcal

MOOLI KANDA
(A Radish Salad)

This is a radish side salad which comes from the state of Himachal Pradesh, India. It usually accompanies the traditional main meal as it provides freshness to the palate and aids in digestion of food.

Serves 4

INGREDIENTS
Red radish thinly sliced – 250 g
Carom seeds – 1 tsp
Lemon juice – ¼ cup
Red chilli powder – ½ tsp
Castor sugar – 1 tsp
Coriander roots – 3 g
Salt to taste

METHOD

Make a dressing with lemon juice, salt, castor sugar, red chilli powder, carom seeds and set aside.

Toss the sliced radish along with dressing and coriander roots.

Keep for at least one day in refrigerator for pickling and consume next day.

Tip: Use the mandolin slicer to slice the radish evenly or it can be grated to infuse the flavours evenly in the dish.

Per serving

Carbs	Fat	Protein	Fiber	Sugar	Sodium
171.75 gms	6 gms	9 gms	8.5 gms	63.75 gms	58 mg

Calories per seving: 352 kcal

Modern Indian Vegetarian Cuisine

SOUPS

Ankurit Dal Aur Tamatar Ka Shorbha .. 42
Matar Pudina Shorbha 45
Ankurit Channa Shorbha 46
Palak Dalchini Shorbha 48
Tomato Coconut Soup 51
Smoky Pumpkin and Mustard Soup ... 52

ANKURIT DAL AUR TAMATAR KA SHORBHA
(Tomato and Lentil Broth)

This soup is healthy, light and perfect to tingle your taste buds. I came up with this idea while working in the kitchen when one of the guests asked for replacement for crouton with a healthier option. Finally, the soup was conceptualised for the event and since then it became a very popular dish on the menu.

Serves 4

INGREDIENTS

Vegetable oil – 1 tbsp
Butter – 15 g
Garlic – ½ tbsp
Shallots chopped – 20 g
Cardamom green – 2-3 no
Cinnamon – 1 small stick
Bay leaf – 2 no
Ginger chopped – ½ tbsp
Coriander roots – 3 g
Sprouted moong dal – 60 g
Tomatoes red ripe – 700 g
Kashmiri chilli powder – ¼ tsp
Vegetable stock – 500 g
Cooking cream – 2 tbsp
Sugar – 1 tbsp
Black pepper crushed – ¼ tsp
Salt to taste

GARNISH
Moong lentil sprouts – 20 g

METHOD

Heat oil in a pan; add butter *(Tip: adding oil and butter together prevents the butter from burning or changing colour)* and stir in the whole spices; as they crackle, add shallots, garlic, ginger and sauté lightly.

Add tomatoes, cut in quarters, and lentil sprouts; season with salt, coriander roots, vegetable stock and Kashmiri chilli powder.

Pressure cook or cover with lid until the tomatoes are done.

Cool the soup mixture and then remove the whole spices.

Blend the soup mixture in a fine blender until it is smooth; strain through fine chinois and make sure you press the chinois to extract maximum juice with minimum waste.

Place the strained soup on the heat and let it simmer, season with sugar, crushed pepper and add cooking cream to enrich the soup.

Garnish with moong sprouts.

Per serving
Calories per seving: 515 kcal

Carbs	Fat	Protein	Fiber	Sugar	Sodium
102.5 gms	10.25 gms	17.25 gms	22 gms	47.75 gms	143.75 mg

Soups

Modern Indian Vegetarian Cuisine

MATAR PUDINA SHORBHA
(Green Pea and Mint Broth)

Green pea and mint shorbha is a wholesome soup which can be served both hot or cold and mint adds freshness to the subtle taste of peas. Mint and peas are a classic combination and is a perfect soup for winters.

Serves 4

INGREDIENTS

Vegetable oil – 1 tbsp
Butter – 15 g
Garlic – ½ tbsp
Shallots chopped – 30 g
Cardamom green – 2-3 no
Cinnamon – 1 small stick
Bay leaf – 2 no
Ginger chopped – ½ tbsp
Green chilli chopped – 1 no deseeded
Coriander roots – 3 g
Green peas – 500 g
Vegetable stock – 500 g
Cooking cream – 1 tbsp
Mint chopped – 1 tbsp
Baby spinach – 60 g
Salt to taste
White pepper to taste

GARNISH

Crème fraiche – 15 g
Mint oil – 1 g

METHOD

Heat oil in a pan; add butter and stir in the whole spices, as they crackle, add shallots, garlic, green chilli, ginger and sauté lightly.

Then add green peas, vegetable stock and season.

Once it boils, remove immediately; add spinach leaves for the colour and mint leaves for flavour.

Cool immediately, and then remove the whole spices.

Blend the soup mixture in a fine blender until very smooth, strain through a fine chinois; make sure you press the chinois to extract maximum juice with minimum waste.

Place the strained soup on the heat and let it simmer season with salt, pepper and add cooking cream.

Garnish with crème fraiche, mint oil and green peas.

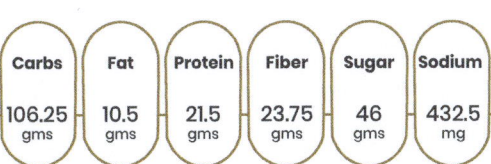

Carbs	Fat	Protein	Fiber	Sugar	Sodium
106.25 gms	10.5 gms	21.5 gms	23.75 gms	46 gms	432.5 mg

Per serving

Calories per seving: 575.75 kcal

ANKURIT CHANNA SHORBHA
(Sprouted Black Gram Broth)

Healthy, wholesome and a nourishing soup, which is a rich source of proteins and fibres with deep flavours of spices.

Serves 4

INGREDIENTS
Vegetable oil – 1 tbsp
Butter – 15 g
Cumin seeds – 1 tsp
Garlic – ½ tbsp
Shallots chopped – 20 g
Cardamom green – 2-3 no
Cinnamon – 1 small stick
Bay leaf – 2 no
Ginger chopped – ½ tbsp
Green chilli chopped – 1 no deseeded
Soaked channa sprouts – 250 g
Tomatoes puree – 4 tbsp
Kashmiri chilli powder – ¼ tsp
Vegetable stock – 600 g
Coriander roots – 4 g
Salt to taste

GARNISH
Sprouted black channa – 20 g

METHOD
Heat oil in a pan; add butter and stir in cumin seeds and the whole spices; as they crackle, add shallots, garlic, green chillies, ginger and sauté lightly.

Add channa sprouts, tomato puree, vegetable stock and then season with salt, coriander roots, and Kashmiri chilli powder.

Pressure cook or cover with lid until it is done.

Cool the soup mixture and remove the whole spices.

Blend the soup mixture in a fine blender until very smooth and strain through fine chinois; make sure you press the chinois to extract maximum juice with minimum waste.

Place the strained soup on heat and let it simmer; check the seasoning again.

Garnish with channa sprouts.

Per serving
Calories per seving: 483.7 kcal

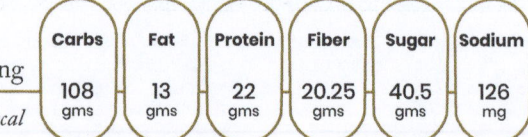

Carbs	Fat	Protein	Fiber	Sugar	Sodium
108 gms	13 gms	22 gms	20.25 gms	40.5 gms	126 mg

Soups

PALAK DALCHINI SHORBHA
(Spiced Spinach Broth)

An iron booster, this recipe makes flavoursome and intriguing bright green soup with a hint of cinnamon. A decadent experience for the senses.

Serves 4

INGREDIENTS

Vegetable oil – 1 tbsp
Butter – 10 g
Garlic chopped – 1 tbsp
Ginger chopped – 1 tsp
Green chillies chopped – 1 tsp
Shallots chopped – 20 g
Spinach leaves washed – 500 g
Vegetable stock – 600 g
Cinnamon whole – 2 sticks
Cream – 2 tbsp
Cinnamon powder – 1 tsp
Salt to taste
Pepper to taste

GARNISH

Spinach leaves – 6 no
Besan flour – 2 tbsp
Corn flour – 1 tbsp
Carom seeds – ¼ tsp
Water – 50 ml
Cherry tomato – 4 no (seasoned oven roasted at 150 degrees C for 1 hr)
Salt to taste
Pepper to taste
Oil to deep fry

METHOD

Heat oil and butter in a pan, add cinnamon stick and shallots, sauté lightly, then add garlic, ginger and green chillies.

Add the vegetable stock and spinach leaves, then season with salt and pepper; once the soup comes to boil, immediately cool the mixture; remove the cinnamon after cooling it.

Blend the soup mixture in a fine blender until very smooth and strain through fine chinois, make sure you press the chinois to extract maximum juice with minimum waste.

Place the soup on heat, finish with cream and a little cinnamon powder.

Check the seasoning and serve hot.

FOR GARNISH

Make a thin batter with besan flour, corn flour, seasoning and carom seeds; dip in fresh spinach leaves and deep fry; immediately keep these on an absorbent paper to drain excess oil.

Garnish with battered-fried spinach leaves and slow-roasted cherry tomato.

Per serving
Calories per seving: 977 kcal

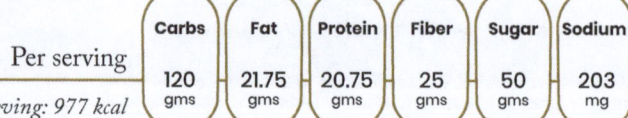

Carbs	Fat	Protein	Fiber	Sugar	Sodium
120 gms	21.75 gms	20.75 gms	25 gms	50 gms	203 mg

Soups

49

Modern Indian Vegetarian Cuisine

TOMATO COCONUT SOUP

A hearty blend of tomato coconut curry leaves and spices to create a culinary delight to sensuate your taste buds. I prefer MTR brand of sambhar masala; however we can use the homemade or preferred bought in product for this recipe.

Serves 4

INGREDIENTS

Vegetable oil – 2 tbsp
Tomato ripe large – 800 g
Garlic chopped – 1 tbsp
Ginger chopped – 1 tbsp
Green chilli – ½ tsp
Onion chopped – ¼ cup
Turmeric powder – ¼ tsp
Curry leaves – 8-10 no
Coriander powder – ¼ tsp
Red chilli powder – ¼ tsp
Cumin powder – ¼ tsp
Coriander roots – 4 g
Coconut milk – 250 ml
Sambhar powder – 1 tbsp
Butter – 20 g
Salt to taste

GARNISH

Oven dried tomatoes – 8 no
(thinly sliced tomatoes dried in the oven at 110 degrees C for 2 hrs)

METHOD

Heat oil; add chopped onions, garlic, ginger, green chillies, curry leaves and sauté until cooked.

Add tomatoes and season, stir in cumin, coriander and red chilli powders along with coriander roots and a little water. Cover and cook the soup until the tomatoes are nicely cooked.

Cool it, and blend the soup mixture in a fine blender until very smooth and strain through fine chinois, make sure you press the chinois to extract maximum juice with minimum waste.

Place the soup extract on heat; add coconut milk, sambhar powder and finish with butter. Check the seasoning.

Garnish with oven dried tomato.

Carbs	Fat	Protein	Fiber	Sugar	Sodium
13.75 gms	13.5 gms	2.75 gms	3.75 gms	6.25 gms	128 mg

Per serving

Calories per seving: 183 kcal

SMOKY PUMPKIN AND MUSTARD SOUP

I discovered this recipe while making a regional dish in Himachal, which involves similar flavours and techniques. I realised that the combination of mustard and pumpkin is delectable. This recipe reflects the rich and hearty traditional flavours.

Serves 4

INGREDIENTS

Vegetable oil – 1 tbsp
Butter – 15 g
Garlic – ½ tbsp
Shallots chopped – 20 g
Cardamom green – 2-3 no
Cinnamon – 1 small stick
Pumpkin yellow peeled and sliced – 300 g
Ginger chopped – ½ tbsp
Green chilli finely chopped – 1 tsp
Vegetable stock – 700 g
Coriander roots – 8 g
Mustard powder – ½ tsp
Jaggery – 1 tbsp
Toasted pumpkin seeds – 1 tbsp
Salt to taste

SMOKING

Charcoal – 1 no
Ghee – 1 tbsp
Cloves – 2 no

METHOD

Heat oil in a pan; add butter and stir in the whole spices, as they crackle, add shallots, garlic, green chilli, ginger and sauté lightly.

Add pumpkin, coriander roots, vegetable stock and season.

Simmer until the pumpkin is cooked; then remove from heat.

Cool immediately and remove the whole spices.

Blend the mixture in a fine blender until very smooth and strain through fine chinois, make sure you press the chinois to extract maximum juice with minimum waste.

Place the strained soup on heat and let it simmer; add mustard powder and season with salt, pepper and jaggery.

SMOKING

Once the soup is done, place it in a deep dish and keep some space to place the charcoal.

Heat a charcoal piece and place ghee and cloves on the hot charcoal; cover the dish to ensure smokiness.

Garnish with toasted pumpkin seeds.

Per serving
Calories per serving: 867 kcal

Carbs	Fat	Protein	Fiber	Sugar	Sodium
95.75 gms	12.5 gms	2.75 gms	17.25 gms	45.25 gms	100.25 mg

Soups

MAIN COURSE

Paneer Dum Anari	57
Mirchi Paneer	58
Gobhi Mussallum	60
Paneer Lavang Latika	63
Kacche Paneer Ke Kofte	64
Aloo Bukhara Kofta	67
Satmooli Ka Saag	68
Karela Khurchan	71
Sepu Vadi	72
Sukki Bhein	75
Chakki Ka Saag	76
Aloo Mandra	78
Kathal Ka Haleem	80
Dal Malai	83
Dal Soya Curry	84
Mahani	87
Surkh Paneer, Pista Korma with Saffron Rice and Crispy Raw Mango and Okra	88
Hariyali Tava Paneer, Achari Khichdi Tikki, Cucumber Raita	92
Saffron Cashew Nut Upma, Murungaikai Rasam, Chctinaad Spiced Potatoes, Keerai Masiyal	96
Sabu Dana Khichdi, Pan Grilled Arbi and Dill Raita	101

Modern Indian Vegetarian Cuisine

PANEER DUM ANARI
(Slow Cooked Cottage Cheese with Pomegranate Seeds)

This is a scrumptious delicacy prepared with thin escalopes or slices of paneer stuffed with pomegranate, cheese and spices. It is finished with silken tomato sauce and slow cooked on dum. A dish, I learnt from Qureshi chefs while working in ITC Hotels. Paneer slicing involves good technique as they have to be carefully rolled, filled with spiced mixture and pomegranate seeds and simmered in silken pomegranate tomato sauce without a tear.

Serves 4

INGREDIENTS
Paneer block – 500 g

STUFFING
Processed cheese grated – 100 g
Coriander chopped – 2 g
Ginger finely chopped – 1 tsp
Mint chopped – 2-3 leaves
Pomegranate seeds – 20 g
Chaat masala – ¼ tsp
Mace powder – 1 pinch
Cardamom powder – ¼ tsp
Salt to taste

SAUCE
Makhni sauce – 800 g
Beetroot juice – 20 g
Pomegranate juice – 20 g
Garam masala – ¼ tsp
Butter – 30 g
Salt to taste

METHOD
Oven roast the paneer at 180 degrees C for 10 mins.

Prepare the stuffing by mixing all the ingredients together.

Cool the paneer block and prepare very thin slices using a mandolin or a very sharp knife.

Arrange the slices on the table and put the stuffing inside the paneer and roll.

Arrange the rolls neatly on the tray ensuring the end of the roll is facing towards the tray to avoid it from opening and set aside.

SAUCE
Heat makhni sauce and add strained beetroot and pomegranate juice to it, reduce until it becomes thick and then season.

Finish with garam masala and knob of butter.

Lightly heat the paneer rolls in the oven at 180 degrees C for 10-15 minutes (this process helps in heating the paneer and also binds the stuffing to the paneer) and pour the sauce on the paneer.

Garnish as desired.

Carbs	Fat	Protein	Fiber	Sugar	Sodium
21 gms	58.25 gms	9.5 gms	15 gms	3.75 gms	1,199 mg

Per serving

Calories per seving: 611 kcal

MIRCHI PANEER
(Cottage Cheese Stuffed Chillies)

While trying new dishes at home and surprising my family, I came up with this idea, chilli and fresh cottage cheese are cooked together in the dish and it can be served as a snack or in sauce. Here I have used sauce blend to compliment the chilly stuffed paneer. As this a perfect fuse of pungent chillies, soft paneer and aromatic flavours from the spices, it is an exquisite dish to tingle your palate.

Serves 4

INGREDIENTS

Green large chilli – 3 no
Red large chilli – 3 no

MARINADE FOR CHILLIES

Olive oil – 2 tbsp
Chaat masala – 1 tsp
Salt to taste

STUFFING

Paneer/Fresh chenna – 80 g
Chopped ginger – 2 g
Chopped coriander – 2 g
Chaat masala – 1 tsp
Processed cheese grated – 40 g
Salt to taste

COATING OF CHILLIES

Paneer/Fresh chenna – 200 g
Cornflour – 1 tbsp
Salt to taste

SAUCE

Brown sauce – 600 g
Butter – 20 g
Cream – 1 tbsp
Garam masala – ¼ tsp
Kasuri methi powder – ½ tsp
Salt to taste

METHOD

Wash the chillies, slit and remove the seeds; marinade the chillies and leave for 3-4 hrs.

Prepare the stuffing by mixing all the ingredients.

Completely mash the fresh chenna ensuring there are no lumps.

Add seasoning and corn flour to bind the chenna and fill the chillies completely with this mix and coat with chenna cornflour mixture.

Arrange the chillies on a baking tray and cook for 10 mins at 170 degrees C in the oven, ensure that the chenna sticks to the chillies.

SAUCE

Heat the brown sauce and enrich it with cream and butter.

Sprinkle garam masala, kasuri methi powder and then season.

Arrange hot chilli coated with chenna on a plate and pour the sauce around it as a garnish as desired and serve hot.

Per serving
Calories per seving: 459 kcal

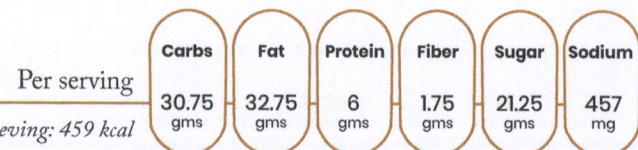

Carbs	Fat	Protein	Fiber	Sugar	Sodium
30.75 gms	32.75 gms	6 gms	1.75 gms	21.25 gms	457 mg

GOBHI MUSSALLUM
(Slow Cooked Whole Cauliflower with Spices)

A modern presentation to traditional recipe of small cauliflower florets marinated and slow cooked with a nutty sauce. Easy to cook and a delight for vegetarians.

Serves 4

INGREDIENTS

Whole cauliflower floret – 4 no (small size)
Turmeric powder – ¼ tsp
Chaat masala – 1 tsp
Lemon juice – 20 g
Salt to taste
Oil to deep fry

SAUCE

Vegetable oil – 2 tbsp
Ginger garlic paste – 1 tbsp
Yoghurt full cream whisked – 100 g
Tomato puree – 100 g
Coriander powder – ½ tsp
Cumin powder – ¼ tsp
Turmeric powder – ¼ tsp
Kashmiri red chilli powder – ¼ tsp
Gram flour – 1 tbsp
Fried onion paste – 50 g
Fried cashew nuts paste – 50 g
Cardamom powder – ¼ tsp
Garam masala – ½ tsp
Cinnamon powder – ¼ tsp
Rose water – 2 g
Kewra water – 2 g
Saffron strands – 8 no (pounded with rose water)
Sugar – 5 g

METHOD

Trim the cauliflower by cutting all the sides.

Boil water with turmeric and salt; boil the cauliflower until it is slightly tender.

Remove the cauliflower and throw away the water.

Deep fry the whole florets on medium heat and set aside.

Season with chaat masala, lemon juice and salt.

SAUCE

Heat oil, add ginger garlic paste and once it is cooked, add yoghurt and spice powders; then add the tomato puree and cook until the oil separates.

Add onion paste, cashew nuts paste and gram flour, cook a little.

Add water to adjust the consistency.

Add the powdered aromatic spices (cinnamon, cardamom and garam masala), and rose, saffron and kewra water.

Add sugar to balance the sourness from the tomatoes.

Check seasoning and ensure that the sauce is not thin, it has to be slightly thick.

Arrange the cauliflower on a baking dish and pour the sauce over it and bake at 180 degrees C for 15 mins.

Once removed from the oven, arrange on a platter and garnish with pomegranate seeds, almond flakes and crushed cashew nuts.

Per serving

Carbs	Fat	Protein	Fiber	Sugar	Sodium
25.75 gms	32.75 gms	10.25 gms	5.75 gms	9.75 gms	127.5 mg

Calories per serving: 378 kcal

Main Course

GARNISH

Pomegranate seeds – 10 g

Almond flakes – 5 g

Crushed cashew nuts – 10 g

Modern Indian Vegetarian Cuisine

PANEER LAVANG LATIKA
(Cloved Cheese Delight)

This dish is very popular in North India as it has paneer filled with spiced khoya and processed cheese studded with cloves and finished in a makhni sauce.

Serves 4

INGREDIENTS

Paneer block – 500 g

Cloves – 12 no

STUFFING

Processed cheese grated – 80 g

Coriander chopped – 2 g

Ginger chopped – 1 tsp

Khoya fresh mashed – 40 g

Chaat masala – ¼ tsp

Clove powder – 1 pinch

Cardamom powder – ¼ tsp

Salt to taste

SAUCE

Makhni sauce – 800 g

Garam masala – ¼ tsp

Kasuri methi powder – ¼ tsp

Butter – 30 g

Salt to taste

METHOD

Oven roast the paneer at 180 degrees C for 10 mins.

Prepare the stuffing by mixing all the ingredients together.

Cool the paneer block and slice very thin using a mandolin or a very sharp knife.

Arrange the slices on the table and put the stuffing inside the paneer and roll and seal with one piece of clove.

Arrange the rolls neatly on the tray and set aside.

SAUCE

Heat the makhni sauce and reduce until it becomes thick, then season.

Finish with garam masala, kasuri methi and a knob of butter.

Pour the sauce on the tray and lightly heat the paneer rolls in the oven at 180 degrees for 10-15 mins (this process helps in heating the paneer and also binds the stuffing to the paneer).

Arrange the paneer neatly on the plate and pour the sauce around it.

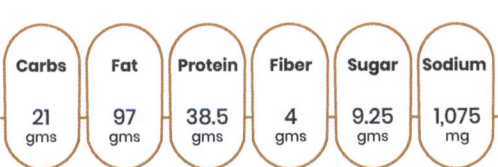

Carbs	Fat	Protein	Fiber	Sugar	Sodium
21 gms	97 gms	38.5 gms	4 gms	9.25 gms	1,075 mg

Per serving

Calories per serving: 5,080 kcal

KACCHE PANEER KE KOFTE
(Cottage Cheese Dumplings)

A sweet dish, kaccha gulla inspired me to prepare the dish. This savoury dish made with fresh chenna or cottage cheese with saffron sauce looks like a dessert, but tastes like a savoury dish.

Serves 4

INGREDIENTS

DOUGH
Fresh chenna – 600 g
Corn flour – 80 g
Chopped ginger – 1 tsp
Chopped green chilli – 1 tsp
Chopped coriander leaves – 3 g
Cardamom powder – 1 tsp
Salt to taste

STUFFING
Potatoes fried mashed – 150 g
Chaat masala – ¼ tsp
Yellow chilli powder – ¼ tsp
Lemon juice – 1 tbsp
Almond flakes – 10 g
Coriander roots chopped – 3 g
Green chillies chopped – 1 g
Ginger chopped – 4 g
Salt to taste

SAUCE
White sauce – 600 g
Saffron – 6-7 no (lightly broiled and powdered in mortar pestle mixed with rose water)
Rose water – 1 tbsp
Cream – 100 g
Cardamom powder – ¼ tsp
Salt to taste
White pepper to taste

GARNISH
Almond slivers – 5 g
Silver vark – 2 no

METHOD

Mash the chenna with the palm of your hands; add all the ingredients to make the dough. Divide the kofta into equal size dumplings and set aside.

Prepare stuffing by mixing all the ingredients and check seasoning.

Stuff the dumplings with the spiced potato mixture and roll using fingers and palm of your hands to round shape; avoid getting any cracks on the surface

Garnish with almonds on top.

FOR SAUCE

Prepare and heat the white sauce as per the recipe and once it starts to simmer adjust consistency by adding water, if so required.

Stir in the spice powders, saffron, rose water and cream and adjust the seasoning.

Place all the koftas on a tray and bake at 170 degrees C for 10 mins.

Pour the sauce around the kofta.

Garnish with almond slivers and silver vark and serve hot.

Carbs	Fat	Protein	Fiber	Sugar	Sodium
39.25 gms	104 gms	10.75 gms	7.75 gms	2 gms	767 mg

Per serving

Calories per seving: 1,082 kcal

ALOO BUKHARA KOFTA

This recipe uses aloo bukhara or dried plums, which have a unique sweet and sour taste when stuffed in paneer and potato mixture, and finished in a creamy, rich cashew nut sauce.

Serves 4

INGREDIENTS
Paneer grated – 300 g
Boiled potatoes grated – 300 g
Refined flour – 30 g
Corn flour – 15 g
White pepper to taste

STUFFING
Processed cheese grated – 80 g
Dried plums or aloo bukhara – 5 g
Ginger chopped – 4 g
Green chilli chopped – 1 g
Coriander chopped – 2 g
Salt to taste
Oil to deep fry

SAUCE
White sauce/gravy – 400 g
White pepper to taste
Cardamom powder – ¼ tsp
Cream – 50 g
Salt to taste

GARNISH
Dried prunes

METHOD

Mash the paneer and potato completely to ensure there are no lumps; season and set aside.

Prepare the stuffing by mixing all the ingredients.

Stuff the dough of potato and paneer with the cheese stuffing and mould them into oblong shapes; ensure there are no lumps in the kofta.

Rest the koftas for a minimum of 1 hr in the refrigerator and then deep fry these on medium heat until golden.

FOR SAUCE

Prepare the sauce as per the recipe and gently simmer over low heat season and then add cream; adjust the consistency by adding water, if required.

Add cardamom powder and seasoning.

Arrange the koftas in a bowl and pour the sauce; garnish with chopped dried prunes.

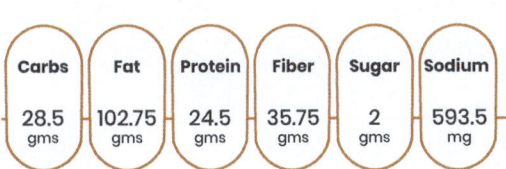

Per serving
Calories per serving: 691 kcal

Carbs	Fat	Protein	Fiber	Sugar	Sodium
28.5 gms	102.75 gms	24.5 gms	35.75 gms	2 gms	593.5 mg

SATMOOLI KA SAAG
(Asparagus with Tempered Spinach)

Not many of us know that asparagus in Hindi is called satmooli. I clearly remember it, as I was asked this question during my final year campus interview. I could not answer then, but I reached out to a chef for the answer. The inspiration for this dish came from the use of healthy crunchy asparagus with a blend of dill leaves and spinach.

Serves 4

INGREDIENTS

Vegetable oil – 2 tbsp

Cumin seeds – ½ tsp

Chopped onions – ¼ cup

Garlic chopped – 1 tbsp

Ginger chopped – 1 tbsp

Green chilli chopped – 1 tsp

Dill leaves chopped – 5 g

Spinach blanched and chopped – 400 g

Spinach blanched and pureed – 200 g

Butter – 20 g

Cream – 2 tbsp

Asparagus whole – 300 g

Butter – 1 tbsp

Salt to taste

METHOD

Heat the oil and then add cumin seeds; once it crackles, add chopped onions; cook until it is translucent, stir in ginger, garlic and green chillies.

Once the garlic is cooked, add dill leaves and stir in chopped spinach, lightly sauté and then add spinach puree; cook a little and season; finish with butter and cream.

Cut the asparagus into equal size dices and discard the stringy stem and keep the asparagus spears for garnish.

Heat water, add salt and quick blanch the asparagus by adding to hot water for 3 mins and chilling under ice water.

Heat the pan and add butter; as the butter melts, add asparagus and season.

Add disced asparagus to the saag; use the asparagus spears as garnish and serve hot.

Per serving

Calories per serving: 228 kcal

Carbs	Fat	Protein	Fiber	Sugar	Sodium
10.25 gms	14.75 gms	6 gms	4.25 gms	2.74 gms	632.25 mg

Main Course

KARELA KHURCHAN

Karela or bitter gourd is a very healthy vegetable, but not relished by everyone owing to its bitter taste. In this recipe, I have made it colourful and also tastier with a combination of other vegetables.

Serves 4

INGREDIENTS

Bitter gourd/karela – 800 g
Turmeric powder – 1 tsp
Salt to taste
Oil to deep fry

SAUCE

Vegetable oil – 1 tbsp
Onions sliced – 100 g
Red pepper sliced – 50 g
Yellow pepper sliced – 50 g
Capsicum sliced – 50 g
Garlic chopped – 0.25 g
Ginger juliennes – 4 g
Onion-tomato masala – ½ cup
Chaat masala – 1 tsp
Amchur powder – ½ tsp
Cumin powder – ¼ tsp
Roasted fennel powder – 1 tsp
Garam masala – ½ tsp
Coriander chopped – 2 g
Salt to taste

METHOD

Peel the skin of bitter gourd and remove the seeds; cut into thick juliennes.

Rub the bitter gourd with salt and turmeric and set aside for 2-3 hrs or until the bitter juices of the gourd are removed.

Deep fry these thick juliennes and set aside.

Heat oil in a pan, add the onions, cook until translucent then add chopped garlic and sauté lightly; stir in the red and yellow pepper, ginger and fried bitter gourd.

Add the onion-tomato masala to nap the karela and sprinkle powdered spices.

Check the seasoning; finally add chopped coriander as garnish and serve hot.

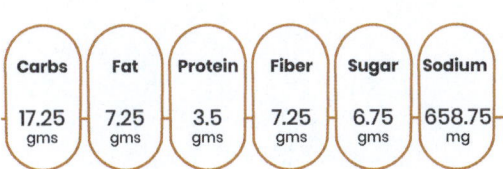

Per serving

Carbs	Fat	Protein	Fiber	Sugar	Sodium
17.25 gms	7.25 gms	3.5 gms	7.25 gms	6.75 gms	658.75 mg

Calories per seving: 317 kcal

SEPU VADI

(Lentil Dumplings in Spinach Sauce)

The dish comes from Mandi district of Himachal Pradesh and lesser known to people from different regions. This recipe will not only make you aware but also it just might become your favourite dish.

Serves 4

INGREDIENTS

Urad chilka dal – 250 g soaked wt
Crushed pepper – 1 tsp
Hing or asafoetida – 1 pinch
Oil to deep fry
Salt to taste

SAUCE

Vegetable oil – 2 tbsp
Cumin seeds – ¼ tsp
Ginger paste – 1 tbsp
Garlic paste – 1 tbsp
Coriander powder – 1 tsp
Green chilli paste – 2 g
Yoghurt whisked – 150 g
Fennel seed powder – 1 tsp
Asafoetida (hing) – 1 pinch
Spinach blanched puree – 300 g
Garam masala – ½ tsp
Cooking cream – 30 ml
Salt to taste

METHOD

Wash the lentil 8-10 times until the water is clear, soak it for 7-8 hours.

After soaking, wash the lentil again and grind to a paste by adding very little water as the texture needs to be coarse and thick.

Add crushed peppercorns and salt. Take a deep container and line the pan with oil and pour the mixture in the pan.

Steam the lentil mixture for 20-25 mins until it is cooked.

Remove the lentil cake from the pan and cut into desired shape – squares, rectangle, cylindrical, etc.

Heat oil in a *kadai* (pot) and deep fry on low heat until golden and the lentil vadi is cooked inside out.

SAUCE

Heat oil in a pan, add cumin seeds; after it crackles, add ginger garlic paste; once its cooked, stir in the powdered spices, green chilli paste, hing and whisked yoghurt.

Cook the yoghurt and once the oil starts to separate on the sides of the pan, add the spinach puree, season and finish with garam masala and cream.

Soak the vadis in hot water before using and squeeze the water when ready to use; finally add to the sauce.

Check the seasoning and serve hot.

Per serving
Calories per serving: 452 kcal

Carbs	Fat	Protein	Fiber	Sugar	Sodium
48.75 gms	24.25 gms	23.75 gms	4.75 gms	1.75 gms	273 mg

SUKKI BHEIN
(Dry Lotus Roots)

Bhein is known by many different names – lotus root, nadru and kamal kakri. It has a nice crispy texture which makes it versatile for culinary use. We have used it to make a dry vegetable coated with aromatic and flavourful spices. I was inspired by my wife's grandmother who taught me this dish and it is now definitely one of my favourites.

Serves 4

INGREDIENTS

Lotus stem peeled and sliced – 550 g

Turmeric powder – ¼ tsp

Vegetable oil – 4 tbsp

Ginger chopped – 1 tbsp

Garlic chopped – ½ cup

Gram flour – ¼ cup

Cumin powder – ¼ tsp

Turmeric powder – ½ tsp

Amchur powder – 1 tbsp

Fennel powder – 1 tsp

Garam masala – ¼ tsp

Kasuri methi powder – ¼ tsp

Chopped coriander – 3 g

Ghee – 50 g

Salt to taste

METHOD

Boil the lotus stem slices in salt and turmeric water until cooked; strain the water and keep them separately.

Heat oil in a pan; add the chopped ginger, garlic and cook until light golden; then add gram flour and powdered spices, except the garam masala and kasuri methi.

Once the gram flour starts cooking and gives out a nice, cooked aroma, add the lotus slices and fold in the mixture; then add chopped coriander, garam masala, ghee and kasuri methi.

Check the seasoning and serve hot.

Carbs	Fat	Protein	Fiber	Sugar	Sodium
37 gms	29.5 gms	8 gms	2 gms	2.5 gms	127 mg

Per serving

Calories per serving: 507 kcal

CHAKKI KA SAAG

This dish comes from Rajasthan, its taste and texture are just like meat, which comes from the gluten of the wheat. I have used the gluten to serve as main course, however it has versatile uses and can be an excellent starter if prepared by marinating and roasting.

Serves 4

INGREDIENTS

Kneaded whole wheat flour dough – 500 g (made from whole wheat flour 350 g and 140 ml water)

Oil to deep fry

SAUCE

Vegetable oil – 2 tbsp
Ginger paste – 1 tbsp
Garlic paste – 1 tbsp
Hing/Asafoetida – 1 pinch
Whole red chilli – 2 no
Tomato puree – 50 g
Yoghurt – 400 g
Gram flour – 30 g
Turmeric powder – ¼ tsp
Kashmiri chilli powder – ¼ tsp
Coriander seeds crushed – 1 tsp
Cumin powder – 1 tsp
Cooking cream – 30 ml
Garam masala – ¼ tsp
Kasuri methi – ¼ tsp
Coriander chopped – 2 g
Salt to taste

METHOD

Wash the dough in running water, keeping the strainer underneath to collect the gluten.

After 5-10 mins, a dough with texture like net will be formed which is gluten from the flour.

Collect all the left gluten and shape it into small size balls and boil.

Remove from water and deep fry the dough balls, and immediately soak in warm salted water.

SAUCE

Heat oil in a pan, add the ginger garlic paste and sauté; then add hing and whole red chilli; sauté lightly.

Add tomato puree and stir in the powdered spices except garam masala.

Separately mix the gram flour to yoghurt slowly by continuously whisking it to make a smooth batter.

Add the whisked yoghurt to the gram flour and continuously cook, and stir until the mixture comes to boil, add little water if required to adjust the consistency of the sauce.

Check the seasoning and cook until oil comes on top.

Assemble by adding the dumpling to the sauce.

Finish with garam masala, kasuri methi and cream; finally add chopped coriander.

Per serving
Calories per serving: 677 kcal

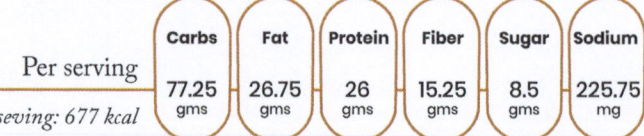

Carbs	Fat	Protein	Fiber	Sugar	Sodium
77.25 gms	26.75 gms	26 gms	15.25 gms	8.5 gms	225.75 mg

ALOO MANDRA

A very popular dish from my hometown Kangra Valley, Himachal Pradesh, and a must try for vegetarians. This dish is made without garlic, onion or tomato. It is usually made with chickpea or paneer, however here I have added my twist by using the sauce as base for stuffed potatoes.

Serves 4

INGREDIENTS

Potatoes large – 6 no
Oil for frying

STUFFING

Grated cheese – 60 g
Cashew nuts crushed – 15 g
Coriander roots chopped – 3 g
Lemon juice – ½ tbsp
Chaat masala – ½ tbsp
Raisins – 10 g
Green chilli chopped – 1 tsp
Salt to taste

SAUCE

Vegetable oil – 2 tbsp
Whole black cardamom – 1 no
Green cardamom – 3 no
Bay leaf – 1 no
Khoya grated – 30 g
Turmeric powder – ½ tsp
Coriander powder – 1 tsp
Chilli powder – ½ tsp
Yoghurt – 3 cups
Gram flour – 1 tbsp
Ghee – 3 tbsp
Sugar – 1 tbsp
Salt to taste

METHOD

Take potatoes, peel them using a peeler or a scooper to make a hole in the centre for the filling; keep the trimmings on the side. Do not throw them away.

Fry the potatoes inside out until nice and golden; then fry the trimmings.

Make the stuffing by mixing all the ingredients and fried trimmings.

Once the potatoes are cooled, stuff the potatoes and set aside.

SAUCE

Heat oil in a pan; add whole spices and as they splutter, add khoya. Sauté until its cooked, then add the powdered spices and stir in whisked yoghurt with a pinch of gram flour *(Tip: gram flour is just added to avoid the yoghurt from splitting)*.

Season and keep stirring until the sauce starts to boil; then add ghee and simmer the sauce on low heat.

Add sugar to balance the sourness from yoghurt and cook until the oil and ghee comes on top.

Pour the sauce over the potatoes and serve hot.

Note: If khoya is not available, you can use full cream in the same quantity.

Per serving
Calories per seving: 1,335 kcal

Carbs	Fat	Protein	Fiber	Sugar	Sodium
116.26 gms	40.5 gms	22.25 gms	15.25 gms	17.25 gms	100.75 mg

KATHAL KA HALEEM

Haleem is a popular dish from Hyderabad made from meat. Haleem is a wholesome food which has lentil, starch and protein all in one meal. In this recipe, I have used jackfruit to make a wholesome vegetarian delight.

Serves 4

INGREDIENTS
Jackfruit peeled diced – 800 g
Oil to deep fry

PASTE
Urad dal white – 50 g
Channa dal – 30 g
Rice basmati – 20 g
Broken wheat – 50 g
Salt to taste

SAUCE
Vegetable oil – 3 tbsp
Cardamom whole – 3 no
Cinnamon whole – 2 no
Sliced onions equal size – 200 g
Ginger garlic paste – 2 tbsp
Yoghurt whisked – 250 g
Yellow chilli powder – 1 tsp
Coriander powder – 1 tbsp
Green chillies finely chopped – 1 tsp
Mint leaves – 10-12 no
Chopped coriander – 2 tbsp
Garam masala – 1 tsp
Salt to taste

TEMPERING
Ghee – 3 tbsp
Lemon juice – 1 tbsp
Sliced onions –200 g

FOR GARNISH
Lemon wedge
Green chilli
Fried onions
Ginger jullienes
Mint
Coriander

METHOD

Fry the jackfruit dices on low heat until completely cooked and golden in colour.

Take the fried jackfruit pieces and cut the shredded part; then keep aside to be used later; make a fine paste of the pulp left after removing the shredded jackfruit. (Once fried, the shredded jackfruit has a similar texture as that of meat.)

FOR PASTE

Wash the rice, lentils and broken wheat mix 3-4 times and soak in water for at least 1 hr.

Boil lentils, rice and broken wheat along with salt. Once it is cooked, strain the mix and cool. Make a fine paste of this mix and keep separately.

FOR THE SAUCE

Heat the vegetable oil in a heavy bottomed pan, add whole cardamom and cinnamon.

Once the spices are brown, add sliced onions and cook until golden brown; then add the ginger garlic paste and sauté until cooked.

Add yellow chilli powder, coriander powder and season; stir in the yoghurt and keep cooking until the oil separates.

Add the dal paste and jackfruit paste to the pan and continuously stir and cook it together until it gets nice light golden colour. The texture of the mix should be slimy and add little water to adjust the consistency, if so required, then at this stage, add the shreds of jackfruit to the mixture.

Add chopped green chillies, chopped coriander and mint; finish with garam masala.

TEMPERING

Heat ghee in a separate pan, add sliced onions, cook until golden brown and pour on Haleem.

Add lemon juice to it and serve hot with traditional accompaniments of sliced green chillies, mint, ginger, fried onions, lemon wedges and chopped coriander.

Carbs	Fat	Protein	Fiber	Sugar	Sodium	
121.75 gms	33.5 gms	34.75 gms	44.25 gms	53 gms	541 mg	Per serving
						Calories per serving: 668 kcal

DAL MALAI
(Creamy Tempered Lentil)

A white lentil curry was prepared while cooking for a VIP banquet event and for that we needed to do something special and different. The lentil or dal is quite flavourful and royal treat for vegetarians.

Serves 4

INGREDIENTS

Urad dal white – 300 g
Milk – 300 g
Water – 500 g
Salt to taste

TEMPERING

Vegetable oil – 30 g
Onion chopped finely – 150 g
Garlic finely chopped – 30 g
Ginger finely chopped – 30 g
Green chillies finely chopped – 3 g
Lemon juice – 5 g
Ghee – 20 g
Cooking cream – 20 g
Salt to taste

GARNISH

Coriander finely chopped – 4 g
Silver varq – 1 no

METHOD

Wash urad dal 3-4 times and soak for minimum of 30 mins before cooking

Boil the dal with salt and water, add milk once it is partially cooked. Once fully cooked, set aside.

TEMPERING

In a separate pan heat oil and add evenly chopped onion; cook till its translucent and then add garlic, ginger; cook until light golden colour is seen then add green chillies; pour this mix over the boiled dal and gently mix lemon juice.

Pour ghee and cream on the dal and mix the cream to enrich the dal.

Garnish with silver leaf and coriander leaves.

Tip: This dal does not have any spices, all flavour come from onions, garlic, ginger and chillies; ensure the onions, garlic and ginger are evenly cut and cooking is done to right colour and texture.

Carbs	Fat	Protein	Fiber	Sugar	Sodium
62.75 gms	12.75 gms	22 gms	22.75 gms	3 gms	71 mg

Per serving
Calories per serving: 381.5 kcal

DAL SOYA CURRY
(Dill Flavoured Lentil)

A melange of two types of lentils tempered with dill leaves and spices. Comfort family food which can be relished with rice or bread. This, lentil curry recipe was given to me by Mr Gautam Anand in ITC. I tried it for a special function in Delhi and thereafter it became very popular and has been a must have for every function since then.

Serves 4

INGREDIENTS

Masoor dal – 200 g
Moong dal – 200 g
Vegetable oil – 2 tbsp
Cumin seeds – 1 tsp
Finely chopped garlic – 1 tbsp
Finely chopped ginger – 1 tbsp
Finely chopped green chilli – ½ tsp
Turmeric – ½ tsp
Red chilli powder – ½ tsp
Dill leaves chopped – 30 g
Ghee – 2 tbsp
Coriander leaves chopped – 2 g
Salt to taste

METHOD

Wash the lentils under cold running water, then place in a deep pan and cover with four times its volume of water. Leave to soak for 20 mins, then bring to the boil. Reduce heat, cover and simmer until the lentils are soft and broken down, skimming off any scum from the surface; add more water, if necessary, to prevent the lentils sticking to the base of the pan.

Heat the vegetable oil in a separate pan and add the cumin seeds. As they begin to splutter, add garlic, ginger and green chilli.

Sauté till the garlic begins to colour lightly, then add turmeric, red chilli powder and dill leaves, cook for 2 mins, then pour the mixture over the lentils, add chopped coriander leaves.

Season with salt and stir together well. Add ghee, adjust the seasoning and serve hot.

Per serving
Calories per serving: 399.5 kcal

Carbs	Fat	Protein	Fiber	Sugar	Sodium
44.5 gms	17.5 gms	19.5 gms	12.75 gms	3.25 gms	151.25 mg

MAHANI

An excellent vegan dish traditionally from my hometown and a delight for vegetarians. Black channa simmered to perfection in a sweet and sour sauce. I have shared the basic recipe however; it has various versions depending on the regions and ingredients. Traditionally amchur powder is used in the dish, which comes from raw mangoes grown in Kangra valley. It is dark in colour and has a different taste to commercial brands. However, still the shop bought amchur may be used to make the dish.

Serves 4

INGREDIENTS

Black gram with shell, soaked overnight – 1 cup

Mustard oil – 2 tbsp

Cumin seeds – 1 tsp

Fenugreek seeds ground/powder – ¼ tsp

Green chilli slit – 2 no

Chilli powder – ¼ tsp

Mango powder dried (amchur) – 2 tbsp

Coriander powder – 2 tsp

Fennel seeds (saunf) – 1 tsp

Chickpea flour (besan) – 2 tbsp

Asafoetida (hing) – 1/8 tsp

Water – 3 cups

Coriander leaves chopped – 2 tbsp

Dates dried slivered – 2 0g

Jaggery – ½ tsp

Salt to taste

METHOD

Boil the soaked black gram in a pressure cooker or a pot with lid until it is tender. Drain the grams, but do not throw the liquid.

Heat mustard oil; as it begins to smoke, remove from heat and let it cool to the right temperature of cooking (this technique helps in reducing the pungency of mustard); then add cumin, fenugreek, chilli powder, coriander powder, fennel seeds and chickpea flour to the pot.

Cook until you can smell the toasty chickpea flour; add black gram, asafoetida, green chilli and dates; add the amchur powder and left-over water from the strained black gram, cook till the curry is slightly thick, then add jaggery to balance the sourness.

Simmer the sauce till you get the desired consistency; then check for seasoning.

Garnish with coriander leaves.

Note: Traditionally mango powder comes from Kangra region of Himachal; it is a bit dark in colour and its intense flavour makes the dish wholesome and delicious.

Carbs	Fat	Protein	Fiber	Sugar	Sodium
45.75 gms	12.5 gms	18.25 gms	24 gms	18 gms	429 mg

Per serving

Calories per serving: 425 kcal

SURKH PANEER, PISTA KORMA WITH SAFFRON RICE AND CRISPY RAW MANGO AND OKRA

This concept dish is a complete meal in a bowl. I have used Awadhi flavours that complement each other. It creates a royal feast for the vegetarian diners.

SURKH PANEER, PISTA KORMA

Serves 4

INGREDIENTS

Paneer cut 6 cm x 6cm (60 g each) – 8 pieces

MARINATE

Kashmiri chilli paste – 2 tbsp

Salt to taste

Oil – 2 tbsp

Ginger garlic paste – 1 tbsp

Garam masala – 1 tbsp

INGREDIENTS

PISTA KORMA SAUCE

Oil – 3 tbsp

Ginger garlic paste – 1 tsp

Whole cardamom – 2 no

Mace – ¼ tsp

Pistachio green – 50 g

Cashew nut broken – 50 g

Red onion peeled roughly diced – 200 g

Baby spinach washed – 80 g

Green chilli – 1 no

Cooking cream – 2 tbsp

METHOD

Make marinate and apply over the paneer, set aside for minimum 4 hrs.

Cook the paneer on both sides on a grill.

SAUCE

Heat oil in a large pan over medium heat; add garlic and ginger pastes and sauté for a minute until its cooked.

Add cashew nut, pistachio, onions, cardamom, green chilli, mace, salt and three cups of water; pressure cook or in a pot with lid until cooked. Cool the mixture; add spinach leaves and blend to fine puree.

Heat the blended puree and stir continuously to avoid sauce sticking to the base. Add white pepper, ground cardamom, cumin powder, garam masala and rose water; then season. Simmer for 4–5 mins, until the sauce thickens.

Per serving
Calories per seving: 758 kcal

Carbs	Fat	Protein	Fiber	Sugar	Sodium
21.75 gms	60.5 gms	29.9 gms	4.7 gms	11.2 gms	72.5 mg

Main Course

Cumin powder – ½ tsp
White pepper powder – 1 tsp
Cardamom powder – 1 tsp
Garam masala – ½ tsp
Rose water – 1 tsp
Salt to taste

Add cream and a little water, if necessary, to get the sauce to a pouring consistency.

Remove from heat and serve with paneer.

SAFFRON RICE

Awadhi delicacy of basmati rice cooked with saffron and enriched with cream and ghee.

Serves 4

INGREDIENTS

Basmati rice – 2 cups
Cloves – 2 no
Bay leaf – 2 no
Salt to taste
Milk – ¼ cup
Ghee – 1 tbsp
Water – 2 cups
Saffron broiled and pounded – 6-7 no
Rose water – 1 tsp
Cardamom powder – 1 tsp

METHOD

Wash basmati rice and soak for at least 30 mins in cold water.

Heat ghee in a pot; add bay leaves, cloves and as they crackle, stir in the raw rice; fill with water and milk mixture until the rice is covered; stir in cardamom powder and then cook.

Add salt and saffron.

As soon as the water comes to boil reduce the heat and cover with lid for 10 mins.

Open the lid after 20 mins and serve hot.

Per serving
Calories per seving: 70.75 kcal

Fat	Protein	Fiber	Sugar	Sodium	Carbs
71.5 gms	5.2 gms	0.25 gms	0.75 gms	1 mg	7.50 gms

KHASTA KAIRI BHINDI
(Crunchy Crispy Ladyfinger or Okra)

I learnt this dish during my time with the ITC chefs, where instead of using dry mango powder we tried using raw mango and the result was excellent. The crispy texture of the dish was perfect to add character to the plate.

Serves 4

INGREDIENTS

Ladyfinger, thinly trimmed sliced – 400 g

Gram flour – 4 tbsp

Raw mango peeled thinly sliced – ½ cup

Carom seeds – ½ tsp

Corn flour – 1 tbsp

Red chilli powder – 1 tsp

Lemon juice – 1 tbsp

Asafoetida – ½ tsp

Chaat masala – 1 tsp

Salt to taste

Oil to deep fry

METHOD

Prepare ladyfinger and raw mango slices.

Mix together all the powdered spices, gram flour, corn flour, carom seeds, salt and lemon juice.

Then add little water so that the mixture has the right coating consistency.

Dip the ladyfinger and mango slices and deep fry until crisp and golden; drain on kitchen paper.

Sprinkle chaat masala in the end.

Carbs	Fat	Protein	Fiber	Sugar	Sodium
22 gms	15.75 gms	4.75 gms	1.25 gms	3.25 gms	29.5 mg

Per serving

Calories per serving: 292 kcal

HARIYALI TAVA PANEER, ACHARI KHICHDI TIKKI, CUCUMBER RAITA

(Cottage Cheese in a Green Herb Marinade and Grilled on Tava)

Paneer itself is very bland and absorbs the taste of the marinade. I learnt this dish and developed it further while working for the airlines where we had to place all the main course components in one plate, thus making it sumptuous and a wholesome treat.

HARIYALI TAVA PANEER

Serves 4

INGREDIENTS

Paneer cut into 8 x 60 g – 480 g

GREEN MARINADE

INGREDIENTS

Ginger garlic paste – 4 tbsp

Coriander roughly chopped – 500 g

Mint leaves roughly chopped – 50 g

Green chilli – 2 no

Vegetable oil – 50 ml

Thick hung yoghurt or Greek yoghurt – 50 g

Salt to taste

METHOD

Place all the ingredients for the marinade in a blender or food processor; blitz to form a coarse herb dressing.

Pour this over the paneer and massage gently. Leave to marinate in the fridge for minimum 4-6 hrs.

Pan grill the paneer on hot grill ensuring the paneer and marinade is cooked and serve hot.

Per serving
Calories per seving: 1,342 kcal

Carbs	Fat	Protein	Fiber	Sugar	Sodium
468 gms	125.75 gms	309.75 gms	352 gms	112 gms	353 mg

Main Course

ACHARI KHICHDI TIKKI

Pickled spices, tempered rice shaped into a patty and crumb fried, this dish was developed especially for the airlines' business class section. The meal retains all its moisture, which thus compliments the flavour of other components. A tip I would like to share that when we fly in an aircraft our taste buds are supressed, therefore we need to design food which is moist and full of flavours.

Serves 4

INGREDIENTS

Basmati rice – 90 g
Yellow moong dal – 120 g
Vegetable oil – 30 g
Cumin seeds – 1 tsp
Onion seeds – ¼ tsp
Fennel seeds – ½ tsp
Carom seeds – ¼ tsp
Red onion chopped – 100 g
Chopped ginger – 10 g
Chopped garlic – 1 tbsp
Coriander chopped – 1 tsp
Green chilli chopped – ½ tbsp
Turmeric powder – 1 tsp
Coriander powder – 1 tsp
Garam masala powder – ½ tsp
Red chilli powder – ½ tsp
Water – 450 g
Ghee – 1 tbsp
Grated cheese – 40 g
Salt to taste
Refined flour slurry for crumbing
Panko crumbs to crust
Vegetable oil to deep fry

METHOD

Wash the rice and dal and soak for about 15-20 mins.

Heat oil in a pan, add cumin seeds, onion seeds, fennel seeds and carom seeds; as soon as it begins to crackles, add chopped onions and cook until light golden. Then add chopped ginger, garlic and green chillies; cook until garlic is cooked, stir in the soaked rice and lentil mixture along with the powdered spices.

Add water, season and stir in ghee; cover the pot and cook for about 15-20 mins until rice and lentil are overcooked. Cool the rice khichdi.

Take the cold khichdi portion; add grated cheese and chopped coriander to the mix, then shape it into equal sized patties around 70-80 g each.

CRUMBING

Make the slurry of refined flour and dip each patty crust with the panko crumbs.

Continue the same process for rest of the khichdi.

Deep fry and set aside for assembly.

Per serving
Calories per seving: 420 kcal

Carbs	Fat	Protein	Fiber	Sugar	Sodium
20.25 gms	30.75 gms	5.25 gms	2.75 gms	2 gms	143 mg

Main Course

CUCUMBER RAITA

I always try and use thick yoghurt for making any sort of raitas as it prevents water separation while maintaining its consistency.

Serves 4

INGREDIENTS

Hung yoghurt or thick Greek yoghurt – 200 g

Cucumber peeled and finely diced – 80 g

Coriander chopped – 2 g

Salt to taste

METHOD

Mix all the ingredients, adjust the seasoning as required.

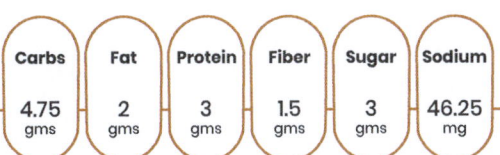

Per serving

Calories per seving: 74.5 kcal

SAFFRON CASHEW NUT UPMA, MURUNGAIKAI RASAM, CHETINAAD SPICED POTATOES, KEERAI MASIYAL

Saffron upma, bharwan aloo, chettinad spice, keerai masial sauce and rasam shots; this is a contemporary style of plating while matching northern and southern flavours on a plate.

SAFFRON CASHEW NUT UPMA

Serves 4

INGREDIENTS

Ghee – 1 tbsp

Mustard seeds – 1 tsp

Curry leaves – 10 no

Finely chopped fresh ginger – 1 tsp

Finely chopped green chilli – ½ tsp

Turmeric – ½ tsp

Semolina – 60 g

Boiling water – 200 ml

Roasted crushed cashew nuts – 2 tbsp

Saffron water – 2 tbsp

Coconut milk – 1 tbsp

Unsalted butter – 1 tbsp

Double cream – 1 tbsp

Lemon juice – 1 tbsp

Salt to taste

METHOD

Heat ghee in a pan and add mustard seeds; as they crackle, add curry leaves, ginger and green chilli; sauté for 1 min.

Add semolina and turmeric powder and sauté until it gives off a nutty aroma; do not allow the colour to change.

Season with salt; add boiling water and whisk until the mixture has the consistency of porridge.

Add crushed cashew nuts and saffron water.

Just before serving, adjust the seasoning and finish by stirring in coconut milk, butter, cream and lemon juice.

The upma should be creamy and quite soft.

Per serving

Calories per seving: 207 kcal

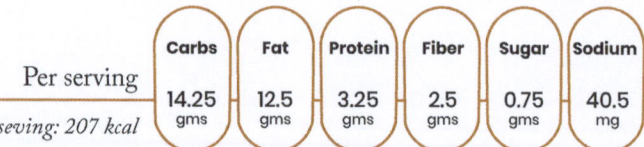

Carbs	Fat	Protein	Fiber	Sugar	Sodium
14.25 gms	12.5 gms	3.25 gms	2.5 gms	0.75 gms	40.5 mg

Main Course

MURUNGAIKAI RASAM

This is an invigorating lentil broth with drumsticks. This is one of the recipes, I learnt at ITC while working with Master Chef Shankaran in Dakshin Restaurant.

Serves 4

INGREDIENTS

Vegetable oil – 2 tbsp

Bay leaf – 1 no

Cinnamon stick – 2 no

Green cardamom – 2 no

Cloves whole – 2 no

Kal pasi (lichen flower) – 2 g

Star anise whole – 1 no

Cumin seeds – 1 tsp

Pepper corns – ½ tsp

Whole coriander – ½ tsp

Green chilli – 5 no

Coriander roots – ¼ cup

Curry leaves – 8 no

Tomato chopped – 200 g

Tamarind pulp – 50 g

Asafoetida – ½ tsp

Chilli powder – 1 tsp

Turmeric powder – 1 tsp

Coriander powder – ½ tsp

Tur dal – 1 cup

Drumsticks – 6 no (cut into 3 inch pieces)

Onion chopped – 125 g

Water – 1.5 lt

Salt to taste

METHOD

Heat oil in a pot and crackle the whole spices including cumin.

Add green chilli, curry leaves, onions, asafoetida and chopped tomatoes; stir continuously, once the tomatoes are cooked; add all the dry spices followed by tamarind pulp.

Add water, bring it to a boil and cook until tamarind is cooked.

Add the drumstick pieces, coriander roots, dal and season.

Simmer the broth until the lentil and vegetables are cooked perfectly.

Strain it and the dish is ready to serve.

Per serving

Calories per serving: 719 kcal

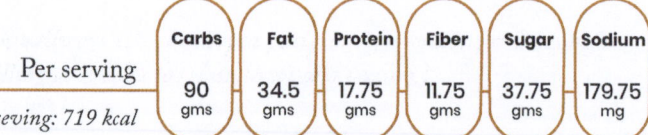

Carbs	Fat	Protein	Fiber	Sugar	Sodium
90 gms	34.5 gms	17.75 gms	11.75 gms	37.75 gms	179.75 mg

CHETINAAD SPICED POTATOES

The dish is definitely not an authentic one, but I tried to use one of my favourite spice mixes, the Chetinaad masala to flavour the potatoes.

Serves 4

INGREDIENTS

Potatoes large – 6 no
Oil for frying

STUFFING

Grated cheese – 60 g
Cashew nuts crushed – 15 g
Coriander roots chopped – 3 g
Lemon juice – ½ tbsp
Chaat masala – ½ tbsp
Raisins – 10 g
Chetinaad spice mix – ½ tsp
Green chilli finely chopped – 3 g
Curry leaves powder – 2 g
Salt to taste

METHOD

Select equal size large potatoes preferrable Haldwani or new potatoes.

Peal and scoop the potatoes to make a hole in the centre.

Fry these on low to medium heat until crisp; do the same with the trimmings.

Prepare the stuffing with left over fried trimmings and the above ingredients by mixing them without any lump formation; then stuff this in the potatoes.

The potatoes are sliced and served.

Carbs	Fat	Protein	Fiber	Sugar	Sodium
59.57 gms	21.25 gms	17.25 gms	14.75 gms	7.25 gms	166.5 mg

Per serving

Calories per seving: 656 kcal

KEERAI MASIYAL
(Tempered Spinach with Lentil)

While working in Delhi ITC in 2006, I was fortunate to taste the culinary delights of South India and learnt more about their cuisine. More than the taste of dosas and idlies, I relished a dish prepared with spinach, lentil and wholesome spices; one of my favourites, and something I wanted to share with my readers.

Serves 4

INGREDIENTS

Spinach leaves blanched and chopped – 600 g

Spinach blanched and pureed – 200 g

Moong dal boiled paste – 300 g

Oil – 2 tbsp

Ginger chopped – 1 tbsp

Garlic chopped – 1.5 tbsp

Curry leaves – 8-10 no

Red onion chopped – 1 cup

Cumin seeds – 1 tsp

Green chilli finely chopped – 1 no

Garam masala – ½ tsp

Ghee – 2 tbsp

Salt to taste

METHOD

Heat oil in a pan and add cumin seeds, as they crackle, add curry leaves followed by chopped onion; cook until translucent, then add green chilli, ginger and garlic.

Stir in chopped spinach followed by puree and sauté until cooked; add lentil paste, and a little water to adjust the consistency; finally season.

Finish with garam masala and ghee.

Per serving
Calories per seving: 494 kcal

Carbs	Fat	Protein	Fiber	Sugar	Sodium
31.75 gms	16 gms	11 gms	14.25 gms	3.25 gms	323 mg

Main Course

SABU DANA KHICHDI, PAN GRILLED ARBI AND DILL RAITA

I always used to compare the texture of crumb fried arbi (colocasia) to fish. Here, I have tried to match the flavours and textures of three components to give you an innovative dish.

SABU DANA KHICHDI

I learnt this dish from my wife, who learnt it while she was working in Ahmedabad. She still believes that she prepares it better than me, however I have added a twist to the recipe by adding colours from bell peppers.

Serves 4

INGREDIENTS

Sagoo – 350 g
Vegetable oil – 2 tbsp
Cumin seeds – ½ tsp
Curry leaves – 10 no
Green chilli chopped – 3 g
Peanuts toasted – 20 g
Red bell pepper diced – 20 g
Yellow bell pepper diced – 20 g
Green bell pepper diced – 20 g
Lemon juice – 1 tbsp
Coriander chopped – 5 g
Potato diced boiled – 100 g
Salt to taste

METHOD

Soak sabu dana overnight; however, rinse thoroughly until water turns clear to get rid of the starch. This is an important step to do before you soak sabu dana.

Always use 1:1 ratio of sabu dana and water; so for 1 cup of sabu dana, use 1 cup of water.

Heat oil in a pan, once hot, add cumin seeds and let them sizzle.

Then add the diced potatoes and cook for 3-4 mins.

Add peanuts, green chilli and curry leaves; as the leaves splutter, add coloured capsicum.

Stir in the drained sabu dana to the pan and season.

Do not cook it for a long as it become sticky.

Remove pan from heat, add lemon juice and coriander; toss to combine.

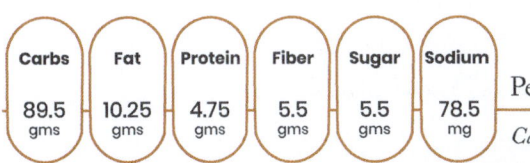

Per serving

Calories per seving: 231 kcal

101

Main Course

PAN GRILLED ARBI

One of my personal favourites, arbi (colocasia) marinated with a spice mix and then crumb fried.

Serves 4

INGREDIENTS
Arbi boiled and peeled – 500 g

MARINATION
Lemon juice – 50 ml
Ajwain seeds – 1 tbsp
Finely chopped green chillies – 1 tsp
Ginger paste – 1 tbsp
Garlic paste – 1.5 tbsp
Salt to taste

FOR CRUST
Refined flour slurry for crumbing
Panko crumbs to crust
Vegetable oil to deep fry

METHOD

Shape the arbi by pressing with hand to resemble small fillet of fish. Prepare marination by mixing all the ingredients.

Marinate the arbi and leave for 2-4 hrs.

Dip them in the flour slurry and then coat in panko crumbs.

Heat oil to 170 degree C in a deep-fat fryer or a deep saucepan, add the arbi and deep fry for about 2 mins, until golden and crisp.

Drain on kitchen paper.

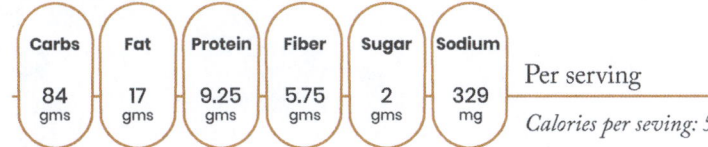

Per serving
Calories per seving: 512 kcal

Carbs	Fat	Protein	Fiber	Sugar	Sodium
84 gms	17 gms	9.25 gms	5.75 gms	2 gms	329 mg

DILL RAITA

Serves 4

INGREDIENTS
Hung yoghurt or thick Greek yoghurt – 200 g
Chopped dill leaves – 3 g
Salt to taste

METHOD
Mix all the ingredients to make the raita.

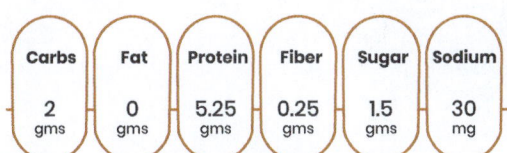

Per serving
Calories per seving: 60.5 kcal

Carbs	Fat	Protein	Fiber	Sugar	Sodium
2 gms	0 gms	5.25 gms	0.25 gms	1.5 gms	30 mg

BREADS

Paanch Anaj Ki Roti 106
Biscuit Roti 109
Papad Nan 110
Warqi Paratha 113

PAANCH ANAJ KI ROTI
(Multigrain Flat Bread)

Indian cuisine has a vast variety of edible healthy flours with high nutritional value. I have combined five flours to get the right texture of the bread.

Serves 10

INGREDIENTS

Whole wheat flour – 150 g
Bajra flour – 100 g
Maize flour – 100 g
Besan – 100 g
Rice flour – 100 g
Desi ghee – 70 g
Milk – 150 ml
Salt to taste

METHOD

Make a soft dough using all the ingredients; just warm the ghee and milk before adding as it helps in making the dough soft.

Rest the dough and divide into equal size balls around 70-80 g.

Roll the dough balls to approximately 10 cm diameter rounds; after rolling, peirce the bread with a fork to ensure it does not puff, thus is gets evenly cooked. Cook on hot griddle or tawa. To make the same bread in tandoor, reduce the ghee quantity to half and once the bread is cooked brush the rest of the ghee on top.

Per serving
Calories per seving: 135 kcal

Carbs	Fat	Protein	Fiber	Sugar	Sodium
20.5 gms	5.75 gms	3.2 gms	1.15 gms	0.4 gms	33.5 mg

BISCUIT ROTI
(Soft Shortbread with Nuts)

I learnt this dish from a casual chef in Moradabad, 2006. The speciality of this bread was that he used to make these in an iron tandoor to make them crisp.

Serves 10

INGREDIENTS
Refined flour – 100 g
Whole wheat flour – 200 g
Semolina or suji – 60 g
Ghee – 60 g
Cardamom powder – ½ tsp
Milk – 60 g
Sugar – 1 tbsp
Salt – ½ tbsp

GARNISH
Almond slivers – 2 tbsp
Pistachio slivers – 2 tbsp
White sesame seeds – 1 tbsp
Ghee for brushing – 20 g

METHOD
Heat milk to luke warm temperature, then add sugar, salt and cardamom powder.

Sieve the flour and mix all these together.

Add ghee to the flour and set aside to rest.

Rub the flour using your fingers and then add the milk mixture slowly to make the dough.

Roll the dough to 1 cm thickness and brush with little water and crust with nuts and sesame seeds.

Cut into desired shape and cook on preheated oven at 180 degree C for 15 mins and immediately brush with ghee and serve hot.

Carbs	Fat	Protein	Fiber	Sugar	Sodium
20.2 gms	8.93 gms	3.73 gms	0.8 gms	1.73 gms	235 mg

Per serving

Calories per seving: 152 kcal

PAPAD NAN

While working in the tandoor section during my initial days as a cook, I always wanted to try something different. It is then that I discovered this recipe while I was trying an experiment – a papad with nan. I cooked both these together at the right temperature, and the combination of the crispy texture of a papad with the soft base of a nan was just scrumptious.

Serves 10

INGREDIENTS

Dried yeast – 7 g
Castor sugar – 2 tsp
Salt – ½ tsp
Warm milk – 2 tbsp
Refined flour – 300 g
Baking powder – ½ tsp
Butter or ghee – 25 g
Natural yoghurt – 30 g
Crushed papad (Lijjat brand) – 1 tbsp
Warm water – 120 ml

METHOD

Mix sugar, yeast and warm milk; set aside until it becomes frothy.

Sieve the flour with salt and baking powder; then mix in the yoghurt to prepare the dough using the frothy mixture.

Cover and leave in a warm place for about 1 hr or until the size is doubled.

Divide it into equal size balls and roll brush with little water and place the crushed papad on top evenly spread throughout the surface.

Cook in the hot tandoor oven until crisp.

Brush with butter while serving it hot.

Per serving
Calories per seving: 198 kcal

Carbs	Fat	Protein	Fiber	Sugar	Sodium
22.6 gms	2.5 gms	4.75 gms	0.5 gms	3 gms	341 mg

WARQI PARATHA

This was the first dough I made when, I entered the dumpukht kitchen as a trainee during my first week. We were asked to make dough for around 10 kg of flour for five bread types. This was a sort of a test to judge the patience level of a trainee whether he/she had it in them to become a chef. I really loved the experience and the challenge while learning that to make this bread, carom seeds were used to enhance the flavours and to make it more digestive. Basically, it is a classic bread that involves technique to make the bread flaky and crisp as it is baked in a clay tandoor.

Serves 10

INGREDIENTS

Refined flour – 1 kg
Carom seed (ajwain) – ½ tbsp
Warm water – 2 cups
Desi ghee – 100 g
Salt to taste

METHOD

Sift the flour, add salt, carom seeds and mix thoroughly.

Make dough with warm water; rest it for a while and then knead again.

Make about 150 g balls of the dough, then roll these into thin flat rounds of about 8 inches diameter.

Apply the melted ghee and fold, cut into equal sized pieces. Keep these on top of each other and press in the middle to stick together.

Rest the portioned dough for a minimum of 30 mins; roll the bread using rolling pin or with your hand and place in hot tandoor. Once cooked, crush the bread with both hands gently to open the layers.

Serve drizzled with ghee.

Tip: The bread can be made on griddle or tawa however, tandoor gives best layers as bread gets cooked at an angle and with gravity all layers open up naturally. Whole wheat flour can be used for a healthier option.

Carbs	Fat	Protein	Fiber	Sugar	Sodium
49.4 gms	7.4 gms	7.3 gms	15 gms	8 gms	7.7 mg

Per serving

Calories per seving: 297 kcal

DESSERTS

Whole Wheat Kasar, Siphon Nimish,
Edible Flowers and Chocolate Chard .. 116
Coconut Kheer with Anjeer Kulfi 119
Adrak Kacchi Haldi Ka Halwa 122
Jamun Ka Meetha 125
Gulab Ki Kheer 126

WHOLE WHEAT KASAR, SIPHON NIMISH, EDIBLE FLOWERS AND CHOCOLATE CHARD

I always felt that the Indian desserts are labour intensive and precise as any other international desserts. While tasting the apple crumble, I always wanted to explore Indian desserts for their texture, therefore I used the kasar for its crumbly texture which I have combined with this amazing dish.

Serves 4

INGREDIENTS

WHOLE WHEAT KASAR

Whole wheat flour – 1 cups
Ghee – 1 tbsp
Sugar, powdered – 1/2 cup
Green cardamom, powdered – 1 tsp

METHOD

In heavy bottomed pan, melt the ghee and add the whole wheat flour; stir-fry over low heat.

As soon as the colour changes to light brown, turn off the heat and leave the mixture to cool completely.

Add sugar and cardamom; mix well.

Per serving
Calories per seving: 247.75 kcal

Carbs	Fat	Protein	Fiber	Sugar	Sodium
49.5 gms	4.25 gms	3.25 gms	1.25 gms	25 gms	1 mg

Desserts

NIMISH

The special chaat uses milk as the main ingredient and is also known as Daulat Ki Chaat. This iconic dish comprises raw milk that is mixed with cream and cooled over an ice slab overnight. After about 8 to 10 hours of cooling, a portion of this is removed and whisked by hand until it is light and frothy. I have used the siphon gun to make this dessert quickly. A mouthlicious dish that can be made throughout the year.

Serves 4

INGREDIENTS

Milk full cream – 1 lt
Double cream – 250 ml
Cardamom powder – 1 tsp
Cream of tartare – 1 tsp
Powdered sugar – 50 g

GARNISH

Almond slivers
Rose petals dried
Pistachio slivers
Chocolate chard
Crushed nougat or chikki

METHOD

Combine milk, cream, cardamom powder, cream of tartar and sugar in a large bowl and refrigerate overnight.

Strain the mixture and pour in siphon gun with cylinder pour, place the new nitrogen cylinder chill and using correct procedure safely, squeeze the foam on top of crumble.

Garnish with edible flowers, nuts, crushed nougat and chocolate chard.

IF YOU DON'T HAVE A SIPHON

Whisk the cold milk mixture after resting for a minimum of 8 hours with an electric mixer on a base of ice cubes; stopping occasionally to remove the froth onto a platter with a wide spoon.

Per serving
Calories per seving: 245 kcal

Carbs	Fat	Protein	Fiber	Sugar	Sodium
12.62 gms	6 gms	4.12 gms	1 gms	0.125 gms	61.12 mg

Desserts

COCONUT KHEER WITH ANJEER KULFI

In Dubai, while working on a Modern Menu, I made a simple kheer using coconut milk, however with the help of the Executive Chef, we combined other components to make it wholesome and presentable for international customers for a fine dining experience.

COCONUT KHEER

Serves 4

INGREDIENTS

Rice broken basmati soaked – 100 g
Milk full cream – 1 lt
Sugar – 150 g
Coconut milk – 300 ml
Cardamom powder – 1 pinch

METHOD

Heat milk in a pot on slow heat, add the pre-soaked rice and cook until it is done and the milk has reduced to half its quantity.

Stir in sugar and as soon as it melts, add thick coconut milk and gently fold into the mixture.

Add a pinch of cardamom spice powder and remove the pot from the heat and chill.

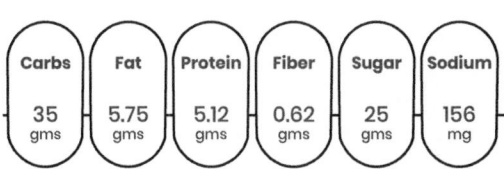

Per serving

Carbs	Fat	Protein	Fiber	Sugar	Sodium
35 gms	5.75 gms	5.12 gms	0.62 gms	25 gms	156 mg

Calories per seving: 342 kcal

ANJEER KULFI

Dry figs provide wholesome energy, and especially when reduced with milk, it is a delight to tantalise the palate.

Serves 4

INGREDIENTS

Milk full cream – 1 lt
Cardamom powder – 2 g
Rose water – 1 tbsp
Dry fig – 100 g (soaked and chopped)
Sugar – 50 g
Almond paste – 40 g
Fresh cream – 50 g

METHOD

Boil the milk and reduce to almost 40% of its original volume.

Strain, cool to room temperature, then add cardamom powder, figs, sugar and almond paste; mix well.

Add fresh cream, mix well and pour into plastic moulds, close with the lid and freeze in an upright position.

GARNISH

Sliced fruit.

Tender coconut sliced.

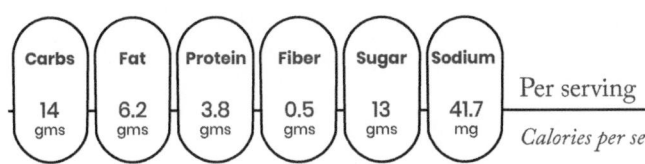

Per serving

Calories per serving: 384 kcal

ADRAK KACCHI HALDI KA HALWA

Going back to history, this dish was made by hakeems to cure cold and cough during winter months. It was during my initials days at ITC, where I learnt that this dish was the most favoured one for winter months.

Serves 4

INGREDIENTS

Ginger paste – 150 g (finely strained after diluting with water)

Fresh turmeric grated – ½ tbsp

Cashew nut paste – 200 g

Khoya (danedar) – 200 g

Milk – 500 g

Cardamom powder – 1 tsp

Jaggery – 180 g

Ghee – 80 g

GARNISH

Almond flakes.
Candied ginger.

METHOD

Put all the ingredients in a heavy bottomed pot except ghee and jaggery; cook slowly until it becomes rich and brown; stirring continuously to avoid burning at least for an hour.

Add jaggery as soon as the colour of the fudge caramelises, then add ghee; keep cooking until it leaves the sides; it will take about 10 mins.

Serve hot; garnish with almond flakes and candied ginger.

Per serving
Calories per seving: 1,144 kcal

Carbs	Fat	Protein	Fiber	Sugar	Sodium
45.7 gms	35.5 gms	14.3 gms	1.6 gms	33.5 gms	265.9 mg

JAMUN KA MEETHA

Indian blackberry or jamun is seasonal and is a good source of vitamin C to strengthen the immune system. While it also reduces inflammation, it is used to treat anaemia and it also acts as a blood purifier. I have created a visual treat by using the berries for making a thick compote. It is excellent when served with ice cream.

Serves 4

INGREDIENTS

Jamun fruit – 2 kg
Water – 1 lt
Sugar – 200 g
Cooking red wine – 50 ml (optional)
Crushed black pepper – 3 g

METHOD

Heat water and add jamun; boil until the berries become tender; remove from water and deseed them.

Add sugar to water and reduce till it becomes thick; add red wine (optional) and spice with little crushed peppercorns.

Add deseeded berries to the thickened sauce and serve warm or cold.

It goes well with ice cream or kulfi.

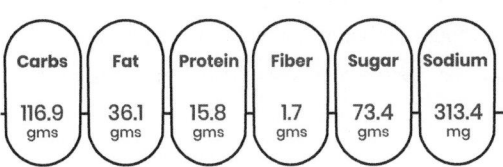

Per serving

Calories per seving: 488 kcal

Carbs	Fat	Protein	Fiber	Sugar	Sodium
116.9 gms	36.1 gms	15.8 gms	1.7 gms	73.4 gms	313.4 mg

GULAB KI KHEER

I distinctly remember this dish, as I learnt it in ITC. Even though it is very simple, however combining flowers with fresh milk and reducing it to perfection with nice aromatic flavours is really amazing.

Serves 4

INGREDIENTS
Milk full cream – 2 lt
Sugar – 80 g
Rose water – 1.5 tbsp
Fresh Rose petals finely sliced – 50 g (musk rose preferably)

GARNISH
Rose gulukand, a bought in product – 50 g
Pistachio powder – 100 g
Silver/gold vark – 1 no

METHOD
Heat milk on a low flame and stir continuously; as it reduces to half, add the rose petals.

On further reduction of milk; add rose water and finish with sugar.

GARNISH
Mix the pistachio and gulukand to form mini balls and coat the balls with silver/gold vark.

Garnish the kheer with these balls and serve chilled.

Per serving
Calories per seving: 571 kcal

Carbs	Fat	Protein	Fiber	Sugar	Sodium
21.1 gms	7.9 gms	6.4 gms	0.1 gms	19.9 gms	86.6 mg

MEASUREMENT TABLE

Spice	Tablespoon 1 tbsp	Teaspoon 1 tsp	Teaspoon ½ tsp	Teaspoon ¼ tsp
Ajwain/carom seeds whole	8.5 g	3 g	2 g	0.7 g
Black cardamom whole	8 g	4 g	2 g	1 g
Coriander whole	5 g	2 g	1.2 g	1 g
Cumin whole	8 g	3 g	2 g	1 g
Fennel seeds whole	10 g	2.5 g	2 g	0.5 g
Fenugreek seeds whole	13 g	5.5 g	3 g	1 g
Kalonji/onion seeds whole	9.5 g	3.5 g	2 g	1 g
Mustard seeds whole	11 g	4.5 g	3 g	1 g
Red chilli whole	5 g	3 g	1.3 g	0.7 g
Shahi jeera / black cumin whole	9 g	3.5 g	2 g	0.7 g
Bay leaf powder	5 g	1.6 g	1 g	0.5 g
Black pepper powder	10 g	4 g	2 g	1 g
Black salt powder	15 g	5 g	3 g	1 g
Chaat masala	13 g	5 g	2.4 g	1.5 g
Chana masala	9 g	3.5 g	2 g	0.5 g
Cinnamon powder	8 g	2.3 g	1.9 g	0.5 g
Cloves powder	5 g	2.3 g	1.5 g	0.7 g

Measurement Table

	Tablespoon 1 tbsp	Teaspoon 1 tsp	Teaspoon ½ tsp	Teaspoon ¼ tsp
Coriander powder	8.5 g	2.5 g	2 g	0.5 g
Cumin powder	10 g	4 g	2 g	0.6 g
Degi mirch powder	10 g	4 g	1.6 g	0.5 g
Garam masala powder	10 g	3.5 g	2 g	0.6 g
Green cardamom powder	9 g	3.5 g	2 g	1 g
Kashmiri chilli powder	10 g	3 g	2 g	0.6 g
Kasuri methi or dry fenugreek leaves (broiled & powdered)	14 g	7 g	3 g	1 g
Mace powder	5.6 g	2 g	1 g	0.5 g
Mango or amchur powder	10 g	3 g	2.1 g	0.7 g
Nutmeg powder	9 g	3.3 g	2.5 g	1 g
Poppy seeds powder	13.5 g	4.5 g	2.7 g	1 g
Red chilli powder	8 g	3.5 g	2 g	0.5 g
Salt	20 g	9 g	5 g	2 g
Turmeric powder	10 g	3 g	2.2 g	0.5 g
White pepper powder	12 g	4.5 g	2 g	1 g
Yellow chilli powder	9 g	3 g	2 g	0.5 g
Oil	**1 cup**	**½ cup**	**1 tbsp**	**1 tsp**
Desi ghee	234.9 g	117.4 g	17.4 g	6.8 g
Groundnut oil	205.4 g	102.7 g	10.8 g	2.8 g
Peanut oil	208.8 g	104.4 g	13.1 g	2.7 g

	1 cup	½ cup	1 tbsp	1 tsp
Refined oil	208.8 g	104.4 g	13 g	3.1 g
Sesame oil	200.7 g	100.35 g	14.2 g	3.6 g
Flour	**1 cup**	**½ cup**	**1 tbsp**	**1 tsp**
Bengal gram flour	124.5 g	62.25 g	8.6 g	3.1 g
Coarse gram flour	139.5 g	69.75 g	11.6 g	3 g
Corn flour	127.8 g	63.9 g	9.2 g	3.5 g
Maida	137.1 g	68.55 g	9.8 g	3.5 g
Maize flour	139.5 g	69.75 g	10.5 g	4.8 g
Roasted channa powder	135.6 g	68.75 g	9.3 g	2.5 g
Semolina or suji fine	182.7 g	91.35 g	13.7 g	5.4 g
Soya flour	137.7 g	68.85 g	10.7 g	4.1 g
Whole wheat flour	133.8 g	66.9 g	11.4 g	3.5 g
Lentil	**1 cup**	**½ cup**	**1 tbsp**	**1 tsp**
Arhar/red dal	213.9 g	106.95 g	20.6 g	7.2 g
Black channa	209.7 g	104.85 g	18.6 g	8.3 g
Black masoor dal	225 g	112.5 g	16.8 g	5.8 g
Black urad dal	208.2 g	103.7 g	19.2 g	6.7 g
Channa dal/split chickpea	201 g	100 g	20.3 g	7.9 g
Chickpea	216.6 g	103.6 g	18 g	7.6 g
Green moong dal	208.2 g	104.1 g	18 g	6.2 g
Kidney bean	180.6 g	90.3 g	17 g	7.7 g

Measurement Table

	1 cup	½ cup	1 tbsp	1 tsp
Red masoor dal	212.4 g	106.2 g	17.3 g	7 g
Split urad dal	200.7 g	100.35 g	20.5 g	5.9 g
Turkish gram	224.7 g	112.5 g	16.8 g	6.2 g
White urad dal	225 g	110 g	10 g	7.5 g
Yellow moong dal	297 g	104.85 g	16 g	7.4 g
Rice	**1 cup**	**½ cup**	**1 tbsp**	**1 tsp**
Basmati rice	192.9 g	36.5 g	14.8 g	6.3 g

GLOSSARY

A

Adrak: another term for ginger.

Ajwain: carom seeds.

Aloo: potato.

Amchoor: dried mango powder; this is added to dishes just before they finish cooking to add a tangy taste.

Arbi: Colocasia, also called the taro root; a starchy vegetable with a nutty flavour.

Asafoetida: dried gum resin of an Indian plant, with a very strong flavour and odour; not to be eaten raw.

Atta: finely ground whole wheat flour is used for making various types of breads.

B

Badam: almond.

Baghar (tempering): spices and herbs are added one at a time to hot oil and this tempering is either done as the first step in the cooking process, before adding the vegetables for example, or as the last, pouring the tempered oil over dal. The oil extracts retain all the sharp flavours of the rai, kadi patta, jeera, hing, etc., and coats the entire dish being prepared. Also known as tadka or chonk.

Basmati rice: this is authentic Indian long-grained white rice, which has a unique nutty flavour. Basmati rice is very popular in India and all over the world. A wide variety of rice dishes are made with it such as plain steamed rice, pulaos, pilafs, biryanis or just different types of fried rice, which may include meat, vegetables, nuts and even fruits at times. Gourmet cooks prefer to use it for its fragrant flavour. During special occasions, dishes are mostly made using this variety of rice.

Baste: moisten food during cooking with fat (melted butter) to prevent the oil from drying.

Bay leaf (Tej patta): pungent dried leaves of the Laurel plant. This is a staple in curries; added to hot oil; they sizzle and release a heady, woody fragrance.

Bhaaji or sabji: any vegetable.

Bhunao (sauté/stir-fry): small quantities of water, yoghurt and stock are introduced to the pan if and when the ingredients start to stick. Usually onions, tomatoes, ginger, garlic and green chillies are fried in oil, but to make sure that this doesn't stick, burn or cook unevenly, a small amount of water is added, repeatedly. After the oil separates from the mixture, the main ingredient (meat or vegetable) is added and cooked.

Broil: method of cooking food using direct heat without any oil or water.

C

Chaat masala: a mixture of dried mango powder, dried pomegranate seeds and black salt used to season and create spicy tangy taste in salads, main courses and drinks.

Chaat: a salty snack served with an array of sweet and spicy chutneys.

Chakki: a machinery to ground fresh flour from all grains.

Chaval: rice.

Chettinad: a cuisine from Tamil Nadu region in India; also used as an aromatic.

Chinois: a conical strainer used to strain sauces and soups.

Chutney: a blend of fruits and spices cooked into a thick sauce. There are sweet-savoury chutneys.

Curry leaves (kadi patta): leaves of a tree which are mostly used when fresh to flavour curries and dry vegetable dishes. It is used extensively in the West and South of India. The dried leaves have hardly any flavour, so buy a bag and freeze to use it for up to six months.

Curry powder: a generic mix of basic Indian ingredients such as turmeric, chilli, coriander and cumin powders.

D

Dal (Dhal): a word used to describe lentils and also the curry made by adding a tempering (*tarka*) to boiled lentils.

Dehydrate: technique to remove water or moisture from vegetables or ingredients.

Dum: a way to steam foods in a pot with a tightly covered lid or a sealed pot. A popular spiced vegetable dish is 'Dum Aloo'. In the olden days, the utensil was sealed with atta (dough) to capture the moisture within the food as it cooked slowly over charcoal fire. Some coal was placed on the lid to ensure even cooking. The food continued to cook in its own steam, retaining all its flavour and aroma. Dum means 'to steam' or 'mature' a dish.

E

Elaichi: cardamom, a spice common in curry blends and garam masala.

F

Fennel seeds (badi saunf): Similar to aniseeds, but longer, more subtle and used in cooking. They have a distinct liquorice-like taste.

Fenugreek (methi): a bitter fragrant plant. The fresh leaves are used as a leafy vegetable. The dried version, known as *kasoori methi*, is soaked in hot water and sprinkled over curries to balance sweet or acidic flavours.

Fenugreek seeds: small flat seeds that are used in curries for slightly bitter flavour; also sold as a dried leaf.

G

Garam masala: literally hot spice; this is a combination of rich and bitter whole spices that are dry roasted and then powdered. Some garam masalas can have up to 33 ingredients but the most common are bay leaves, cinnamon, cloves, green cardamoms and coriander seeds. Avoid the hassle and buy this readymade.

Ghee: clarified butter; it is made by slowly melting butter, skimming off the foam, and saving the golden liquid, leaving the white butter solids behind. This butter can be heated at higher temperatures without burning as compared to ordinary butter. Delicious but also most fattening!

Gram flour (besan): this is chick pea flour. It is used to make the batter for *bhaajis* and is also used in soups and curries. It is gluten free, pale yellow in colour and has a soft fine powdery texture.

Grazing: small amounts of portions.

Greek yoghurt: this is thick and creamy textured yoghurt. It is widely available in Europe, if you live in the US, try a yoghurt with a higher fat content or strain your regular yoghurt in a muslin cloth so it doesn't split when cooking.

Gulkand: sweetened preserve made from rose petals.

H

Halwa: a congealed, translucent sweet dish made of fruits and syrups.

J

Jaggery (gur): dried pieces of unrefined sweet made from sugarcane juice; the most common form of sugar in India; a thick sweet mixture with a texture that ranges from butter to fudge.

Jamun fruit: jamun is an evergreen tropical tree mainly found in India.

K

Kachumber: an Indian salad usually made with small diced cucumber, tomatoes and onions flavoured with salt, sugar and lemon juice. As it goes, with any Indian dish, the varieties can be endless.

Kadai (pronounced kar-hai): a heavy-bottomed wok with two round handles on either side. Dishes cooked in this also bear its name.

Kairi: raw mango.

Kebabs: marinated and spiced small pieces of any meat, poultry, fish, ground meat, vegetables that are skewered or grilled in a tandoor/oven or over a grill. Kebabs can also be shallow fried over a pan.

Kewra water: extract of the pandanus flower, with a heady fruity, rose-like fragrance. It is added for its aromatic punch to sweet and savoury dishes.

Khichadi: a mildly spiced rice and dal preparation. Usually made when you want to eat a light meal or are suffering from a stomach disorder, as it is not only nutritive but can be easily digested.

Khoya: also known as 'mawa', it is made by bringing milk to a boil in a pot and stirring continuously on low flame. It is then reduced and thickened to the consistency of soft cream cheese. It is widely used for making many Indian desserts and sweet meats.

Khurchan: Hindi word for scrape; it is intended to extract all the juices and flavours from the pan to main dish.

Koftas: spiced meat or vegetable balls that can be filled with any type of stuffing.

Korma: a vegetable or meat-based dish cooked in yoghurt and spices-based sauce.

M

Mace (javetri): this is the dry dark outer part of the nutmeg; it has a stronger and more bitter flavour than the nutmeg seed.

Masala dani: a spice box containing commonly used dry spices. It is always kept near the cooking area for easy, quick access. A spoon is included for ease of use.

Masala: spices, herbs and other seasonings ground or pounded together. When wet ingredients like water, vinegar, yoghurt, etc., are added to the spice mixture it is appropriately called a 'wet masala'. Dry spice mixtures are also called 'garam masala' or commonly known in the world as 'curry powder'. Indian cooks generally don't use pre-prepared curry powder – originally a British invention to approximate Indian seasoning – but prefer making their own ever-changing blends.

Mint (pudina): the leaves of the plant are used fresh or dry, in cooking or for chutneys. It is a digestive with a pleasant, cooling quality.

Moong dal: green gram which can be split and de-husked to give an oval-shaped yellow lentil.

Mussalum: any meat, chicken or vegetable cooked slowly whole.

Mustard oil: warm golden orange oil pressed from mustard seeds. Unsurprisingly, this has a sharp and strong flavour.

Mustard seeds: seeds of the mustard plant. You get three varieties – white, brown and black. The black mustard seeds are used widely in cooking.

Mutter: peas.

N

Naan: Indian flat bread made from wheat and baked in a tandoor.

Nigella seeds (kala jeera): known as black onion or black cumin seeds, these are small with a distinct bitter and peppery taste. These are often sprinkled over naans.

P

Paneer: Indian cheese that is rubbery when cold and with a soft, mozzarella-type texture when cooked.

Papad (pappadom in South India): thin wafer like discs about 4-8 inches in diameter made from a variety of lentils, potato, shrimp, rice, etc. The discs are deep fried or dry roasted on an open flame and served as a crispy savoury appetizer. Served in many Indian restaurants as a complimentary dish before a meal.

Paratha: whole-wheat unleavened flatbread. It is sometimes filled with cooked ground meat or a vegetable mixture. Slightly larger than a chapati and shallow fried to perfection.

Pulao: a delicately flavoured rice, sautéed in ghee and seasoned with whole spices like cumin, clove, etc. In Indian cuisine there are many ways in which this pulao can be prepared.

R

Raita: a vegetable and yoghurt dip.

S

Saffron (zafran): the most expensive spice in the world, these are delicate golden red threads. Soak it in warm milk before adding to a dish to get the full power of its rich, musky aroma.

Semolina (rava): grainy, pale-yellow colour flour derived from durum wheat. It has a course texture and is used to make sweet and savoury dishes.

Slurry: it is a mixture of water and flour (corn, besan or wheat).

Star anise: anise flavoured, star-shaped seed pod of a dried fruit. This releases a heady fragrance when added to hot oil.

T

Tamarind (imli): fruits and seeds of the tamarind tree encased in a brown, dry seedpod. Its flesh is extracted as pulp to add a tart, tangy taste to dishes.

Glossary

Tandoor: Indian clay oven used to make speciality foods at high temperatures.

Tawa: heavy-bottomed flat frying pan used to make flatbreads.

Tikka: skewered and tandoor-grilled pieces of meat or vegetable.

Tikki: Hindi name for patty, can be stuffed and usually pan fried.

Turmeric: a bright yellow powdered root similar to ginger plant root. It is used in small quantities to add a soft bitter taste and yellow colour to curries and other dishes.

Upma: a spiced semolina cooked with or without tiny cubed potatoes, peas and sometime shrimp; it is garnished with freshly grated coconut and cilantro.

Urad dal (black lentils): these resemble small black beans and have white interiors. Urad dal has a distinct earthy and thick way about it and is most famously used to make the North Indian kali dal.

Vadi: dumplings made from lentil, flour and spices can be eaten fresh or dried and preserved.

Vark: a fine thin edible silver foil used to decorate or garnish Indian desserts and 'paan'. It has been known to aid in digestion.

Vegetable stock: slow reduction of vegetable offcuts in water to extract maximum flavour and it is then used as base for sauce.

Warqi: a flaky paratha made up of many layers.

Wheat husk: fibre derived from wheat plant, it is a good source of medicines and has great health benefits.

ACKNOWLEDGEMENT

Writing a cookbook is harder than I thought and more rewarding than I could have ever imagined.

None of this would have been possible without my awesome wife Radhika Sood – from cleaning dirty pots to reading drafts – she has stood by me during my every struggle and my steps forward. That is true love!

My mother Sarita Sood who is a great cook and the best person I have known in all my existence. I am thankful for her unconditional love, blessings and her always encouraging and motivational attitude, pushing me to do better and better every day. My father, Suresh Sood, who is an epitome of discipline, kindness and honesty, who bestowed strong values in me and stood as a sturdy guide supporting my decision. My brother Ankur Sud who is and always will be my best friend and the person who knows me the best. A word of appreciation to my mother-in-law Punam Sood, who is a great cook and has supported me to complete my book.

My little daughter Aaradhya who is a real blessing for us and has been very inspirational to help me focus on my work. My family has helped me to translate my professional journey into words, the result of which has been this amazing book.

A special thanks to Diwan Gautam Anand and Chef Manjit Singh Gill for believing in me and sharing their expertise and culinary knowledge that helped me in my professional growth and providing immense support and encouragement to complete this project. I would also like to thank my mentor's Chef Rajkamal Chopra, Chef Martin Braecker and Chef Colin Binmore for their unconditional support as they marked significant achievements in my career, as well as for their endorsements to complete my book.

Writing a book about the story of your life is a surreal process. I am forever indebted to Vandana Bhagra, Manish Purohit and Neena Gupta for their editorial help, keen insight and ongoing support in bringing my recipes to life. It is because of their efforts and encouragement that I have a legacy to pass on to my family and make my daughter proud someday.

Finally, a word of thanks to all those who have been a part of this project, Priya Dogra for her nutritional inputs, Yusuke Sato for a few culinary pictures, and the entire ITC Culinary Team and Dubai Sheraton Culinary Team, it is from here that ideas for some delicious recipes were inspired.

MY JOURNEY IN ARABIC CUISINE

Food is the heart and soul of my essence and after my foray into writing my first book, I look forward to my next one, ***My Journey in Arabic Cuisine***, which will feature authentic cold and hot mezze, rice dishes and popular breakfast options that were inspired during my work experience in Dubai, Abu Dhabi and Qatar. The rich flavourful spices, appetizing rice plates, delicious beverage concoctions used in Arab cuisine are also emphasised in Indian cuisine. My next book is a food lover's delight as it is a result of heavy trading and historical ties between the two regions, and because many South Asian expats live in the Arab States of the Persian Gulf.

Printed in Great Britain
by Amazon